D0313801

THE SCULPTURE
OF MOISSAC

MEYER SCHAPIRO

PHOTOGRAPHS BY
DAVID FINN

THAMES AND HUDSON

Any copy of this book issued by the publisher as a paperback is sold
subject to the condition that it shall not by way of trade or otherwise
be lent, re-sold, hired out or otherwise circulated, without the
publisher's prior consent, in any form of binding or cover other than
that in which it is published and without a similar condition including
these words being imposed on a subsequent purchaser.

First published in Great Britain in 1985
by Thames and Hudson Ltd, London

All rights reserved. No part of this publication may be reproduced or
transmitted in any form or by any means, electronic or mechanical,
including photocopy, recording, or any information storage and retrieval
system, without permission in writing from the publisher.

Printed and bound in West Germany
Designed by Ulrich Ruchti and Robert C. Morrow

*Fig. 1. Moissac,
Church, Detail
of Tympanum:
Head of Christ*

*Fig. 2. Moissac,
Cloister; Capital
of South Gal-
lery: Feast of
Herod; Martyr-
dom of John the
Baptist*

TABLE OF CONTENTS

Fig. 3. Church;
East Wall of
Porch: Detail
Adoration of Magi

Figs. 4, 5
Church; Detail
of East Wall of
Porch: Presenta-
tion in the Tem-
ple

THE SCULPTURES OF
THE CLOISTER
I

INTRODUCTION

The study here undertaken is of the style of the sculptures of the cloister, the portal, and the porch of Moissac.

A catalogue of the sculptures and a description of each face of every capital in the cloister is desirable but cannot be given here. Such a description would almost double the length of this work. A plan of the cloister has been given instead. This, with the photographs reproduced, provides a fair though not complete view of the contents of the cloister. For a more detailed description the reader is referred to the books of Rupin and Lagrèze-Fossat, which lack, however, adequate illustration and a systematic discussion of style or iconography.

In the present work, the postures, costumes, expressions, space, perspective, and grouping of the figures have been described, not to show the immaturity of the sculptors in the process of representation, but to demonstrate that their departures from natural shapes have a common character which is intimately bound up with the harmonious formal structure of the works. I have tried to show also how with certain changes in the observation of nature apparent in the later works, the artistic character is modified.

In the description of formal relations I do not pretend to find the nature of the beauty of the work or its

cause, but I have tried to illustrate by them my sense of the character of the whole and the relevance of the parts to it. These relations occur in apparently simple capitals in larger number than is suggested by analysis. To carry analysis further would require a wearisome restatement and numerous complications of expression not favorable to simple exposition. The few instances given suffice, I think, to illustrate a pervasive character evident at once to sympathetic perception. The particular problem in description was to show a connection between the treatments of various elements employed by the sculptors—to show that the use of line corresponds to the handling of relief, or that the seemingly confused or arbitrary space is a correlate of the design, and that both of these are equally characteristic features of the inherent style.

I find the essence of the style in the archaic representation of forms, designed in restless but well-coordinated opposition, with a pronounced tendency towards realism. Archaic representation implies an unplastic relief of parallel planes, concentric surfaces and movements parallel to the background, the limitation of horizontal planes, the vertical projection of spatial themes, the schematic reduction of natural

Cloister: Detail of Impost Block from Daniel Capital

Fig. 6. Cloister. Pier Relief: St. Paul

1

A, Gothic church of the 15th century with remains of Romanesque nave walls (c. 1115–1130); B, narthex (c. 1115); C, porch (c. 1115–1130); D, tympanum (before 1115); E, cloister (completed in 1100); F, lavatorium (destroyed); G, chapel and dormitory (destroyed); H, refectory (destroyed); J, kitchen; K, Gothic chapterhouse; L, sacristy.

Subjects of the capitals and pier sculptures:

S. W. pier: Bartholomew, Matthew (Figs. 17, 21, 22).

South gallery: 1, Martyrdom of John the Baptist (Fig. 2); 2, birds in trees; 3, Babylonia Magna; 4, birds; 5, Nebuchadnezzar as a beast (Figs. 47, 74); 6, Martyrdom of Stephen (Figs. 48, 92); 7, foliage; 8, David and his musicians (Fig. 79); 9, Jerusalem Sancta; unsculptured pier; 10, Chaining of the devil, Og and Magog (Figs. 58, 72); 11, symbols of the evangelists (Figs. 64, 63); 12, Miracles of Christ; the Centurion of Caphernaum and the Canaanite woman (Figs. 62, 89); 13, the Good Samaritan (Fig. 59); 14, Temptation of Christ (Figs. 38, 84); 15, Vision of John the Evangelist (Figs. 56, 61, 90); 16, Transfiguration (Figs. 60, 88); 17, Deliverance of Peter (Figs. 78, 81); 18, Baptism (Fig. 76).

S. E. pier: Paul, Peter (Figs. 6, 18, 28, 29).

East gallery: 19, Samson and the lion, Samson with the jaw bone (Fig. 94); 20, Martyrdom of Peter and Paul (Figs. 45, 87); 21, foliage; 22, Adam and Eve; Temptation, Expulsion, Labors (Figs. 34, 39, 40); 23, foliage; 24, Martyrdom of Laurence (Figs. 57, 96); 25, Washing of Feet (Fig. 75); 26, foliage; 27, Lazarus and Dives (Figs. 67, 68); 28, dragons; pier: Abbot Durand (1047–1072) (Figs. 12, 13, 20); 29, dragons and figures; 30, Wedding at Cana (Figs. 30, 52); 31, foliage; 32, Adoration of the Magi (Figs. 35, 36); Massacre of the Innocents (Figs. 35, 37); 33, foliage; 34, foliage; 35, Martyrdom of Saturninus (Figs. 43, 46, 53); 36, foliage; 37, Martyrdom of Fructuosus, Eulogius, and Augurius (Figs. 33, 83, 97); 38, Annunciation and Visitation (Figs. 31, 66).

N. E. pier: James, John (Figs. 15, 16, 19).

North gallery: 39, Michael Fighting the Dragon (Fig. 73); 40, birds; 41, foliage; 42, Miracle of Benedict (Figs. 41, 42); 43, birds; 44, Miracle of Peter (Fig. 71); 45, foliage; 46, angels (Fig. 91); 47, Calling of the Apostles (Figs. 50, 51, 85); 48, Daniel in the Lions' Den, Habbakuk (Fig. 69); 49, Crusaders before Jerusalem (Figs. 49, 65); 50, foliage; 51, four evangelists with symbolic beast heads; 52, birds; 53, Three Hebrews in the Fiery Furnace (Fig. 95); 54, Martin and the Beggar, Miracle of Martin (Fig. 54); 55, foliage; 56, Christ and the Samaritan Woman.

N. W. pier: Andrew, Philip (Figs. 14, 23).

West gallery: 57, Sacrifice of Isaac (Fig. 55); 58, angels with the cross (Fig. 44); 59, foliage; 60, birds; 61, Daniel in the Lions' Den (Fig. 86), Annunciation to the Shepherds (Fig. 32); 62, foliage; 63, grotesque bowmen; 64, Raising of Lazarus (Fig. 70); 65, foliage; 66, dragons and figures; pier: inscription of 1100 (Fig. 24), Simon (Figs. 25, 27); 67, Anointing of David; 68, foliage; 69, birds and beasts; 70, foliage; 71, Beatitudes (Fig. 82); 72, lions and figures; 73, Cain and Abel (Fig. 93); 74, foliage; 75, Ascension of Alexander; 76, David and Goliath.

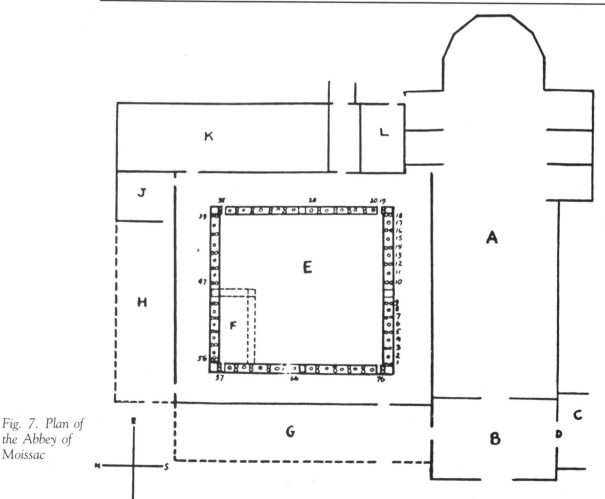

Fig. 7. Plan of the Abbey of Moissac

shapes, their generalized aspect, and the ornamental abstraction or regular succession of repeated elements. In the dominant restlessness are implied unstable postures, energetic movements, diagonal and zigzag lines, and the complication of surfaces by overlapping and contrasted forms, which sometimes compromise the order and clarity inherent in the archaic method. In the movement of arbitrarily abstracted intricate lines, the style is allied with Northern art of the early Middle Ages; in its later search for coordinated asymmetries within larger symmetrical themes it is nearer to the early Baroque of Italy. The realistic tendency, evident in the marked changes in representation in the short interval of thirty years between the cloister and the porch, appears at each moment in the detailed rendering of the draperies, the parts of the body and accessory objects, and in the variety sought in repeated figures.

The earliest sculptures are flatter and more uniform in their surfaces. They are often symmetrical, attached to the wall, and bound up in their design with the architectural frame or surface. Their forms are stylized and their parts more distinct.

In the later works the figures are more plastic and include varied planes. Independent of architecture and bound together in less rigorously symmetrical schemes, they stand before the wall in a limited but greater space. The whole is more intricate and more intensely expressive.

These contrasts are not absolute but relative to the character of the earliest works. Compared to a Gothic or more recent style, the second Romanesque art of Moissac might be described in terms nearer to the first. In the same sense, the first already possesses characteristics of the second, but in a lesser degree and in a somewhat different relation to the whole.

Throughout this work I am employing the term "archaic," not simply with the literal sense of ancient, primitive, or historically initial or antecedent, but as a designation of a formal character in early arts, which has been well described by Emanuel Löwy.[2] In his study of early Greek art he observed a generalized rendering of distinct parts, the parallelism of relief planes, the subordination of modeling to descriptive contours, and other traits which he found also in primitive styles, and explained as characteristics of memory imagery. Although the psychological explanation is not satisfactory and the definition of the features overlooks their positive aesthetic qualities, the description is valuable for the interpretation of mediaeval as well as classic art.

This conception of an archaic style must be qualified and extended in several ways. The archaic characters may be purely conventional formulas (repeating a traditional archaic style), without an immediate origin in the peculiarities of memory or a conceptual reconstruction of a visual whole. In a similar way, they may be aesthetically or morally valued aspects of an early style, consciously imitated by a later artist. In such archaistic works the retrospective character is betrayed by the unconscious and inconsistent participation of the later (often impressionistic) style within the simpler forms.

We must observe also the frequent recurrence, not *survival*, of archaism whenever the untrained or culturally provincial reproduce nature or complex arts or fashion their own symbols; and, on a higher level, when a complex art acquires a new element of representation, like perspective, chiaroscuro, or foreshortening. Thus the earliest formulated examples of parallel perspective in Italian art have the rigidity, simplicity, symmetry, and explicit ornamental articulation of archaic frontal statues, in contrast to the unarchaic complexity of the figures enclosed in this space. In the same sense, in the earliest use of strong chiaroscuro there is a schematic structure of illumination, a distinct division of light from shadow, as in a primitive cosmogony. The archaic nature of the early examples of these elements in highly developed arts is evidenced by the spontaneous reversion to their forms in still later provincial and naive copies of the more recent unarchaic developed forms of perspective and chiaroscuro. The popular ex-votos of the eighteenth and nineteenth centuries often show a perspective and chiaroscuro with the stylistic marks of more skillful earlier art.

Archaic characters are not historical in a chronological sense, except where there is an unilinear development toward more natural forms. The archaic work is conditioned not only by the process of reconstructing part by part the whole of a natural object in imagination, but also by a preexisting artistic representation of it, with fixed characters that are more or less archaic, and by the expressive effects required of the specific profane or religious content. The typology of early Greek art is to some degree independent of the archaic process of designing the types, some of which have been borrowed from Egyptian and Near Eastern arts and have probably influenced the formal result. In a similar way the archaic mediaeval sculptures begin with an inherited repertoire of figure types and iconographic groups of complicated character and also with a preexistent ornament of extreme complexity. These were the forms which had to be reconstructed for plastic representation; the product, though archaic, was necessarily distinct from the classic archaism. Just as the Greek predilection for simple, clearly composed, isolated wholes dominated even the more realistic phases of classic art, the Northern European fantasy of intricate, irregular, tense, involved movements complicated to some degree the most archaic, seemingly clear and simple products of early mediaeval art.

SOME FACTS FROM THE HISTORY OF THE ABBEY

The town of Moissac is situated on the Garonne river, about a mile south of its confluence with the Tarn, in the department of Tarn-et-Garonne. It lies in a strategic position, a crossing point of many roads, some of which were called in mediaeval times "cami-Moyssagues."[3] Traces of Roman habitation survive in classic columns, coins, and fragments of masonry discovered in the town and its surrounding country.[4] The great abbey to which Moissac owes its celebrity was not founded until the middle of the seventh century.[5] A popular tradition has dignified the event by ascribing the foundation to Clovis who was impelled to this act by a dream and divine guidance.[6] Even in the last century the gigantic figure of Christ on the tympanum was called Reclobis by the natives.

The monastery arose under auspicious circumstances, for the diocese of Cahors, to which Moissac then belonged, was ruled by Desiderius, a bishop renowned for both austere living and artistic enterprise.[7] Toward the end of the century the wealth of the abbey was greatly increased by a donation of lands, serfs, and churches by a local nobleman, Nizezius.[8] In the next generations, however, it was a victim of the Saracenic invasion. The church was burned and the surrounding country devastated. Rebuilt in the early ninth century with the aid of Louis the Debonnaire, the abbey suffered a similar disaster at the hands of the Huns and Normans. The reconstructed church was damaged in 1030 by the fall of the roof, and in 1042 by a fire which attacked the whole town. In this period the monastery was harassed by predacious noblemen and the lack of internal discipline. Its abbot, Aymeric de Peyrac, wrote in his chronicle of Moissac (c. 1400) that it had become a "robbers' cave," when Odilo, the abbot of Cluny, passing through Moissac in 1047, effected its submission to Cluny, then the most powerful monastery in Christendom.[9] He placed at the head of Moissac one of his own monks, Durand of Bredon (in Auvergne), under whose administration it acquired

great wealth and prestige. Durand consecrated a new church in 1063[10] and extended his architectural enterprise to the whole region; Aymeric could write that where the boar once roamed the woods now stand churches because of Durand's labors. He was not only abbot of the monastery but also bishop of Toulouse nearby, and upon his death was venerated as a saint by the monks of Moissac. Under the rule of his successor, Hunaud (1072–1085), the monastery acquired vast properties, but was continually embroiled in ecclesiastic controversies and in conflicts with the local nobility.[11] Anquêtil, who followed him, could not ascend his seat without a conflict with a malicious monk. In despair, the usurper set fire to the town; and it was only after a prolonged struggle and papal intervention that Anquêtil's place was finally assured.[12] It is to Anquêtil that we owe the cloister and the sculptures of the tympanum, according to Aymeric's chronicle.[13] But these constructions of Anquêtil were no novelty in Moissac, for works, now destroyed, have been attributed to Hunaud before him,[14] and Durand's architectural energies are well known. Roger (1115–1131) constructed a new church, domed like

Fig. 8. View of the Cloister from South-East Corner

4

those of Souillac and Cahors, and probably added the sculptures of the porch.[15]

This century, immediately following the submission to Cluny, was the happiest in the history of the abbey. It controlled lands and priories as far as Roussillon, Catalonia, and Perigord.[16] In the Cluniac order the abbot of Moissac was second only to the abbot of Cluny himself.[17] Yet the literary and musical productions of this period are few in number. Except for a brief chronicle, a few hymns, and some mediocre verses, the writings of the monks of Moissac were simply copies of earlier works.[18] No monk of the abbey achieved distinction in theology or letters. But in the manuscripts copied in Moissac in the eleventh and twelfth centuries may be found beautiful ornament and miniatures, of which some are related in style to the contemporary sculptures of Aquitaine.[19]

The next century was less favorable to the security of the abbey. In 1188 a fire consumed the greater part of the town which was soon after besieged and taken by the English.[20] And in the subsequent Albigensian crusade the monastery was attacked by the heretics and beset by depressing ecclesiastical and political difficulties.[21] The abbot, Bertrand de Montaigu (1260–1293), repaired some of the damaged buildings, including the cloister of Anquêtil, which he furnished with its present brick arches in the style of the thirteenth century.[22] But in the wars that followed the abbey was again ruined. The church itself was probably subject to great violence, since its upper walls and vaults and its entire sanctuary had to be reconstructed in the fifteenth century.[23]

In 1625 the abbey was secularized and thereafter fell into neglect. The National Assembly, in 1790, suppressed it completely. The church and the cloister were placed on sale; and the latter, purchased by a patriotic citizen, was offered to the town which exposed the building to unworthy uses. The garrison stationed there during the first empire damaged the sculptures and ruined the ancient enameled tile pavements. At one time a saltpeter factory was installed in the surrounding buildings. More recently, as a classified *monument historique*, the cloister and church have received official protection. In the middle of the last century parts of the abbey were restored, but the sculptures were happily left untouched by the archi-

tects of the government.[24]

Since the Middle Ages, the history and arts of the abbey have been the subjects of inquiry and comment. In the late fourteenth century its abbot, Aymeric, in writing his chronicle of Moissac, noted the artistic enterprise of his predecessors and expressed his sense of the great beauty of the Romanesque works. The portal he called *"pulcherrimum, et subtillissimi operis constructum."*[25] He added that the trumeau and the fountain (now destroyed) were reputed so wonderful that they were considered miraculous rather than human works.[26] Aymeric was one of the first of a long line of monastic archaeologists. Not content with the testimony of written documents he made inferences as to the authorship and dates of works from their artistic or physical character. Thus he attributed the unsigned inscription of the dedication of the church of Durand (1063) to Anquêtil, who was not abbot until almost thirty years after, because of the stylistic similarity to the inscription of 1100, placed by Anquêtil in the cloister.[27] On a visit to the priory of Cénac in Perigord, he was struck by the resemblance of its sculptures to those at home in Moissac.[28] He explained them as due to the same patron, Anquêtil, and cited the form of the church as well as written documents in evidence of the common authorship. At other times he was fantastic in his explanations and caused confusion because of his credulity and whimsical statements.

What travelers and artists of the Renaissance thought of the sculptures we do not know.[29] In the seventeenth century scholars, mainly of the Benedictine order, collected the documents pertaining to the mediaeval history of the abbey.[30] De Foulhiac, a learned canon of the cathedral of Cahors, copied numerous charters of Moissac and wrote on the antiquities of Quercy, the region to which Moissac belonged.[31] His still unpublished manuscripts are preserved in the library of Cahors. The monks of St.-Maur, Martène and Durand, who searched all France for documents to form a new edition of the *Gallia Christiana*, and in their *Voyage Littéraire* (1714) described many mediaeval buildings of Aquitaine, did not visit Moissac. The library of the abbey had been brought to Paris about fifty years before.[32] In the later eighteenth century an actor, Beaumenil, on an archaeological mission, made drawings of classical antiquities in Moissac, but paid little attention to the Romanesque works.[33] Dumège, a pioneer in the study of the ancient arts of southern France, wrote a description of the abbey and recounted its history in 1823, in an unpublished manuscript of which copies

are preserved in Moissac and Montauban.[34] It was not until the second quarter of the last century, during the romantic movement in literature and painting, that the sculptures of Moissac acquired some celebrity. In his voluminous *Voyages Romantiques*, published in 1834, Baron Taylor devoted a whole chapter to the abbey, describing its sculptures with a new interest.[35] He drew plans of the cloister and the whole monastic complex and reproduced several details of its architecture. Another learned traveler, Jules Marion, gave a more precise idea of the history of the abbey in an account of a journey in the south of France published in 1849 and 1852.[36] He was the first to utilize the chronicle of Aymeric. In the *Dictionnaire raisonné de l'architecture*, published shortly afterward by Viollet-le-Duc, who had been engaged in the official restorations of the abbey church and cloister, numerous references were made to their construction and decoration.[37] In 1870, 1871, and 1874, a native of Moissac, Lagrèze-Fossat, published a detailed account of the history and arts of the abbey in three volumes.[38] It was unillustrated, and in its iconographic and archaeological discussion suffered from unfamiliarity with other Romanesque works. Other archaeologists of the region—Mignot, Pottier, Dugué, Mommeja,[39] etc.—brought to light details which they reported in the journals of departmental societies. In 1897 appeared Rupin's monograph which offered the first illustrated comprehensive view of the history, documents, and art of the abbey, but was limited by the use of drawings and by the lack of a sound comparative method and analysis of style.[40] In 1901 the Congrès Archéologique of France met in Agen, near Moissac, and devoted some time to the investigation of the architecture of the abbey church.[41] In the following year excavations were made in the nave of the church to discover the plan of the building consecrated by Durand in 1063. Partly because of the infirmity of Monsieur Dugué, the conservator of the cloister, the excavations were never completed, and the results have remained unpublished to this day.[42] In the past twenty-five years the sculptures of Moissac have held a prominent place in discussions of French Romanesque art, but except for the researches of Mâle,[43] Deschamps,[44] and Porter,[45] little has been added to the knowledge acquired in the last century.[46] Deschamps has defined more precisely the relations of the earliest sculptures of the cloister to those of Toulouse, while Porter has shown the extension of similar styles throughout Spain and France and has proposed novel theories to explain the forms at Moissac. In the celebrated work of Mâle on the art of the twelfth century, the sculptures of Moissac are the first to be described. They are for Mâle the initial and unsurpassed masterpieces of mediaeval sculpture, the very inception of the modern tradition of plastic art, and the most striking evidences of his theory of the manuscript sources of Romanesque figure carving in stone. The influence of manuscript drawings on sculptures had long been recognized; it was not until recently that this notion was formulated more precisely. In America, Morey of Princeton had, before Mâle, distinguished the styles of Romanesque works, including Moissac, by manuscript traditions.[47] In Mâle's work the parallels between sculpture and illumination are more often those of iconography.[47a]

THE PIER RELIEFS OF THE CLOISTER

Of the mediaeval abbey of Moissac there survive today the Romanesque cloister, built in 1100; a church on its south side, constructed in the fifteenth century, incorporating the lower walls of the Romanesque church; the tower and porch which preceded the latter on the west; and several conventual buildings to the north and east of the cloister (Fig. 7).[48]

A glance at Figs. 7, 8 will show the reader the rectangular plan of the cloister, the disposition of its arcades with alternately single and twin colonnettes, and the brick piers with grayish marble facings at the ends and center of each arcade.[49]

On the sides of the four corner piers, facing the galleries, are coupled the almost life-size figures[50] of Peter and Paul (southeast), James and John (northeast), Philip and Andrew (northwest), Bartholomew and Matthew (southwest). Simon stands on the outer side of the central pier of the west gallery, facing the garden of the cloister (Fig. 27).[51] On the inner side of the same pier is the inscription that records the building of the cloister (Fig. 24); and on the corresponding side of the central pier of the east gallery, in front of the old chapter house of the abbey, is represented the abbot Durand (1047–1072) (Fig. 13). All these figures are framed by columns, and by arches inscribed with their names.

The rigidity of their postures and their impassive faces, the subdued relief of the hardly emerging figures placed on the shadowy sides of the piers, their isolation at the ends of the galleries, and their architectural frames suggest an archaic funerary art of ceremonious types.

The figures are so slight in relief they appear to be drawings rather than sculptures. This impression is confirmed by the forms of the figures, clearly outlined against the wall, with their features and costumes sharply delineated in simple geometric shapes. The unmodeled bodies are lost beneath the garments which determine the surface design. The costumes are laid out almost flat upon the background and incised with lines in concentric and radial sets like seams or moldings rather than true folds. The different layers of dress lie one upon the other in parallel planes. When folds reach the contour of the figure they stop short, only rarely altering the outline which was conceived before the folds.

It might be supposed from a brief inspection of the piers that the suppression of relief was due to the thinness of the slabs—these are no more than two inches thick—and that an obvious calculation restrained the sculptor. The same hand carving the nearby capitals produced heads and bodies almost completely detached from the stone.

But the character of the relief is not explained by the material alone. The slight projection of the figures was perhaps influenced by the nature of the slab;

Fig. 9. Cloister; Detail of Pier Sculpture: Head of St. Philip

but the limited modeling and shell-like layering of surfaces are independent of it, and may even have favored the use of so thin a slab. With a thicker stone the figures might have been more salient; they would have been no more detached from the wall, and surely no more complex in surface.

In Durand (Fig. 13) the reduced relief, like the symmetry of details, is an essential element of the expressive immobility of the whole. This figure, the only one that is entirely frontal and raises a hand in blessing, is of a commemorative type which retained for a long time an analogous flatness and incised forms.

The relatively greater projection of the figures on the capitals is due to their far smaller size; for size is an important factor in the relief of Romanesque figures. Small sculptures are not simply reduced replicas of large ones; in the adaptations of common types to a new scale, their proportions are modified, the relative thickness of folds increased, and the modeling considerably affected. The more complex architecture of

the capitals, with the salient astragal, volutes, and consoles, (Figs. 32, 33, 36, 37) required as strong an accent of the carved forms, whereas the apostles decorated simple rectangular slabs. The apparently high relief of the small figures on the capitals by the master of the piers includes no greater differentiation of planes or richer modeling.

The reduced relief and simple surfaces are also correlates of the geometrical forms and the linear mode of representation evident throughout the piers. Despite the long tradition of preceding arts, these sculptures share with archaic sculptures of other times a specific manner of conceiving forms.

The body of an apostle is seen in front view, but the head in near profile, and the eye which should gaze to the side is carved as if beholding us. The feet are not firmly planted on the ground, but hang from the body at a marked angle to each other. The thin slab does not determine this trait. On the capitals, where the astragal provides a ledge for feet to stand on, some figures preserve an identical suspension. The movements of the limbs are parallel to the plane of the background. The hands are relieved flat against the bodies, with the palm or the back of the hand fully expanded. The arms are distorted, never foreshortened, and the bent leg is accordingly rendered in profile. The articulation of the body is subordinate to the system of parallel and concentric lines which define the costume. Only at the legs is an understructure of modeled surface intimated, and then only in the most schematic fashion, by a slight convexity of the garment. The folds are rendered as if permanent attributes of the dress, as purely decorative lines, though once suggested by a bodily conformation. They are spun to and fro across the body in regular, concentric, and parallel lines produced by a single incision, or by a double incision which creates a slight ridge, by polygonal patterns of fixed form, and by long vertical moldings parallel to the legs. The folds are curved as if determined by the hollows and salient surfaces of an underlying body. This body is not rendered.

The living details are schematized in the same manner. The head is a diagram of its separate features. The flow of facial surface is extremely gentle; prominences are suppressed and transitions smoothed. Each hair is rendered separately, and bunches of hair or locks form regular spiral, wavy, or imbricated units that are repeated in parallel succession.[52] The eyebrow is a precise arched line, without relief, formed by the meeting of two surfaces.

The eye itself is an arbitrary composition, a regular

Fig. 10. Cloister; Detail of Pier Sculpture: Body of Saint Andrew

object of distinct parts, in simple relation, none encroaching on the next. The lids are treated as two equal, separate members without junction or overlapping. They form an ellipsoid figure of which the upper arc is sometimes of larger radius than the lower, contrary to nature. In some figures (Figs. 9, 17, 19, 20) the eyeball is a smooth unmarked surface with no indication of iris or pupil. In others (Figs. 14, 28, 29) an incised circle defines the iris. The inner corner of the eye is not observed at all.

The mouth shows an equal simplicity. The fine breaks and curves, the hollows and prominences which determine expression and distinguish individuals, are hardly remarked. A common formula is employed here. The two lips are equal and quite similar. Their parting line is straight or very slightly curved, but sharply drawn. In the beardless head of Matthew (Fig. 22) we can judge with what assurance these distortions and simplified forms were produced and how expressive so abstracted a face may be.

A difference of expression is obtained by a slight change in the line between the lips. Drawn perfectly horizontal—Bartholomew (Fig. 17), James (Fig. 19)—the impassivity of the other features is heightened. But in Peter (Fig. 29) it is an ascending line which makes him smile, and in Paul (Fig. 28) a descending line which combines with the three schematic wrinkles of the brow, the slightly diagonal axis of the eye, and the wavy lines of the hair and beard to express a disturbance, preoccupation, and energy that accord well with Paul's own words.

A Romanesque tradition describes Durand as given to jesting, a sin for which he was reproved by the abbot of Cluny and punished after death.[53] The mouth of his effigy has been so damaged that it is difficult to say whether its present expression of malicious amusement is a portrait or an accident of time (Fig. 20). A well-marked line joins the nose and the deep corners of the mouth. The line of the mouth is delicately curved and reveals a search for characterization within the limits of symmetry and patterned geometrical surface.

The drapery forms are as schematic as the eyes and hair. The lower horizontal edge of the tunics of these figures is broken in places by a small unit, usually pentagonal in outline, which represents the lower end of the fluting formed at the base of a vertical fold, or the pleating of a horizontal border. In its actual shape it corresponds to nothing in the structure of drapery, unless we presume that a wind from below has stirred the garment at certain points into this strange schematic fold, and that another force has

flattened it against the body. In the reliefs of James (Fig. 15), Paul (Fig. 6), and Peter (Fig. 18) it appears three times at regular intervals, like an ornament applied to the lower border of the tunic.

We are not surprised to find such forms on figures whose feet hang and whose eyes stare at us even when the face is turned in profile, and whose hands can perform only those gestures which permit us to see their full surface. The elevation or vertical projection of the fold derives from the same habit of mind that gives to objects incompletely apprehended in nature an unmistakable completeness in images. The fold is freed of the accidents of bodily movement and currents which make drapery an unstable system of lines, and is designed instead as a rigid geometrical element. Rather than evoking the free and sporadic appearance of nature, it is further limited, when multiplied, to a few symmetrically arrayed lines.

Similar observations may be made of hands and feet, of the structure of the whole body, and even of the ornaments of the reliefs, the rosettes of the span-

Fig. 11. Cloister; Detail of Pier Sculpture: Detail of Saint Bartholomew

drels, and the foliage of the little capitals.

We must not conclude, like some Greek archaeologists, that material difficulties have determined these peculiarities and that every shape is a compromise of will with a refractory object and inexperience. On the contrary, the material is a fine Pyrenees marble, and the tools were evidently adapted to the most delicate cutting. Only a slight examination of the surfaces will reveal with what care these figures were executed and how thoroughly the sculptor commanded his style. This is observable in two features of the work—the uniformity of execution of repeated elements, and the elegance and variety of detail. The double fold appears a hundred times in these figures, and always with the same thickness and decisive regularity. The forms have been methodically produced; they are not a happy collusion of *naiveté* and a noble model.

The archaism of these works differs from that of early Greek sculptures in an important respect. The pier reliefs contain clear traces of an older, more advanced art: beside the schematic reductions of natural forms there are more complex derivatives of classic naturalistic styles. The profile head is not simply the abstracted contour of a line drawing, as in early Greek reliefs, but is slightly turned to reveal a second eye. This eye is actually foreshortened; it is smaller than the other, and intersects the background wall. It differs from a truly foreshortened eye in its regular form.

Fig. 12. Cloister; Detail of Pier Sculpture of Abbot Durand

Fig. 13. Cloister; Pier Sculpture: The Abbot Durand (1047–1072)

On Simon's head (Fig. 25), which has been turned to a nearly three-quarters view, the profile of the jaw is inconsistent with that turn; it illustrates the domination of a more complex material by an archaic method.[54]

This presentation of the less visible parts of the profile face is to be distinguished from the rendering of the profile head completely in the round on some capitals of the cloister. There no foreshortening is implied, since with the relatively higher relief the entire head could be modeled. The inner eye does not intersect the background wall, nor is there an inconsistent relation of the two sides of the face.

Traces of an unarchaic model are present also in the posture of St. Philip (Fig. 23). Although his feet are suspended as if no ground existed for their support and are parted symmetrically, their point of junction is off the axis of the figure. A line drawn from the sternum to the heels is diagonal and not strictly vertical, as we would expect. This irregularity is balanced by the greater extension of draperies at the right than at the left. The prototype must have been a figure seen in three-quarters view, less rigid than the cloister sculpture.

A more remarkable evidence of originally spatial and plastic prototypes are the pedestals and stairs under the feet of some figures. These pedestals are trapezoidal in shape; they represent foreshortened rectangles, horizontal planes projected vertically in the course of centuries, but retain inconsistently the converging sides. The feet of James (Fig. 15) and of John (Fig. 16) stand on several steps at one time, as if the horizontal bands were a background of the figure and not stairs perpendicular to the wall.

The unarchaic character of the sculptor's prototypes appears also in the costumes of the figures. Whereas the artist seeks distinct forms, a clear patterning and a legible succession of planes, the garments show a complex overlapping and even ambiguity of surfaces. On the figure of Peter (Fig. 18) the end of the mantle on the right shoulder is not continuous with any other piece of clothing; we are at a loss to explain it. The overlapping of drapery at his right ankle is also not clear. Similar inconsistencies occur in the costume of John (Fig. 16); his tunic is covered at the left ankle by the mantle, yet is represented behind the mantle on the background of the relief. The triangular tip of James's chasuble (Fig. 15) is lost in the tunic.[55]

It is already apparent from the description of the small polygonal folds at the lower edges of the tunics that they were simplified versions, not of folds observed

in nature, but of a more plastic expanded form in older art. Classic sculpture had provided the prototypes in the fluttering garments of active figures; these reappear in the stiff immobile apostles in rigid form.[56]

The folds of lambent double curvature across the legs of some figures presuppose a modeling of the body to which they correspond; but this modeling does not exist in the sculptures of the cloister. The form here is vestigial. It betrays its character not only in the association with flat, barely modeled surfaces, but in its actual hardness and sharpness, its doubled line, its uniformity, its pointed termination. These are archaic modifications of an originally fluent fold which moved across a more plastic surface.

The sculptor has evidently reproduced older works of a lesser archaic character, and accepted their complex modeled and foreshortened forms as a matter for schematic reduction in terms of his own linear style. The plausibility of the folds as representations was less important to him than their decorative coherence and clarity as single, isolated rhythmic lines. The apostles as traditional figures received a traditional dress, not subject to verification except in older monuments. In the portrait of Durand, however, the contemporary costume had a symbolic value and was scrupulously drawn, to the last detail. Yet in this figure of the abbot the faithfully rendered forms produce an effect of overlapping and ornamental involvement analogous to the arbitrarily designed garments of the apostles. It is evident that the definiteness of details as single elementary shapes, which governs the archaic process of representation, does not itself determine the character of the whole. We must ask whether the complication of these archaic reliefs is due merely to the reduction of models of ultimately unarchaic, illusionistic character; or whether complex elements of the latter were retained in the process of reduction—which we must suppose took place over a period of several centuries—because of the taste of the reducing artist for a restless and more intricate play of lines. The question may be put in another way: Did a specific method of design and expressive end favor the selection of elements and larger patterns of a complexity exceeding that of the common method of representation?

Before I proceed in the analysis of the design of the reliefs, I shall describe two important kinds of variation in their forms—first, the distinction of individuals by varying details of costume and of face, as well as posture; second, the development evident in the successive renderings of the same element.

The quasi-ornamental rendering of forms shows a realistic bias. If the folds are limited to a few elementary shapes, these are arranged in fresh combinations from figure to figure. The study of the hair alone will reveal the search for variety: in Matthew (Fig. 22) a pattern of hexagonal imbrications, each with parallel vertical lines; in Andrew (Fig. 14) and Peter (Fig. 29), an array of locks ending in small spirals; in Bartholomew, overlaid series of locks with similar spirals (Fig. 17); in Simon, James, and Paul (Fig. 28), long, wavy striations that escape the common regularity; in Philip (Fig. 23) a band of zigzags between the two lower rows of imbricated tufts; and in John (Fig. 16) a row of diagonal hairs emerging from under the ribbed cap. In all these forms, however, there is a common thought. All of them avoid the disordered and accidental in hair and abstract its uniformity of structure; they render its curly, straight, or wavy character by a parallel striation of similar locks or tufts. The forms representing the different kinds of hair remain equally regular and ornamental.

A similar variety is evident in the costumes and accessories of the figures. John alone has a cap; Peter and Paul are sandaled, Durand and Philip wear shoes; the others are barefoot. Some carry closed books, Matthew and Simon have open inscribed volumes,

Fig. 14. Cloister; Detail of Pier Sculpture: St. Andrew

Fig. 15. Cloister; Pier Sculpture: St. James

Fig. 16. Cloister; Pier Sculpture: St. John

James a scroll, Andrew a cross. Even the pedestals of the figures are varied. Under John and James the horizontal bands suggest a staircase, while beneath the others has been carved a quadrangular plaque.

This diversity is not iconographic—a rendering of attributes of the apostles—except in a few details like the cross of Andrew and the inscription of Matthew's book. Is is more probably a character of the style, and accords with an unmistakable tendency toward individualizing representation evident also in slight anatomic variations, some introduced perhaps in the course of the work from figure to figure.

The forms of the human body and its costume are not equally accessible to the archaic method of representation. The artist who did not observe the human eye correctly and misproportioned the arms and legs and head was very careful to represent the stitching in the shoes of St. Andrew (Fig. 14) and each separate hair of his beard. For hairs and stitching are regular, repeated, simple shapes, whereas an eye is asymmetrical, and the proportions of the limbs are unique, unmarked on the body, and not susceptible to a precise ornamental construction.

It is conceivable that these larger or more complex

Fig. 17. Cloister; Detail of Pier Sculpture: Head of St. Bartholomew

parts of the figure should be subject in time to a canonical definition as precise and regular as the simpler elements. Such a regulation and schematic control are familiar to us from Egyptian art.

But in the cloister piers the proportions and details of the figure are not rigorously fixed; and we may perceive within the ten reliefs evidence of observation newly made in the course of work. This is hardly apparent in the modeling of the body, which is everywhere minimized. But proportions change. Bartholomew and Durand are exceedingly short; their heads are little more than one-fifth their total height. In other apostles the heads are one-sixth, and in Peter and Paul approach one-seventh the height of the figure.

The greater breadth of the relief perhaps accounts for the squat proportions of Durand. He stands under a segmental arch instead of the semicircle of the others. Not all the figures are compactly fitted in their frames. Philip, John, and James raise and narrow their shoulders as if to pass through a close archway.

The extreme shortness of the arms of Bartholomew, which recurs in Andrew and Peter, is corrected in Matthew and James.

It is difficult to decide whether these variations proceed from a closer attention to nature or from varying models. The rendering of the iris in Peter, Paul, and Simon might suggest a fresh observation by the sculptor, were it not that the iris appears in Toulouse[57] in earlier sculptures, less naturalistic than the works in Moissac, and is absent from later sculptures that are even more detailed and veracious in rendering the figure.[58]

But in the representation of the ear, we can follow a development which parallels that of early Greek art.[59] In Peter, Matthew, Simon, and Durand, it is small and set too high; in Bartholomew (and Simon) it is more accurately placed, but still too small; in James, however, it is so well observed that, except for the rest of the figure, it might seem by another sculptor. Shapes as well as proportion and position are developed; the parts of the ear become more clearly differentiated.

The variation of the size and shape of the three polygonal folds of the lower edges of Peter's tunic (Fig. 18) reveals a similar tendency. On Andrew's garment (Fig. 14) a diagonal doubled line is incised on the corresponding border to mark the turned-up or folded edge. The ornament of beads and lozenges, common to the costume of James and Durand, is more plastic in the former. In the case of Durand the lozenges are quite flat; in James they are convex and enclose a central jewel.

That these variations indicate a tendency in one direction is impossible to demonstrate by a study of the figures in their original succession in time; for it is not known in what order the figures were carved; and any order inferred from the variation of a single feature, like eyes, proportions, or inscriptions, is contradicted by study of another. The greatest number of uncial characters appears in the inscription of Bartholomew, who is one of the shortest of the apostles and has been considered the most archaic.[60] Except in the relief of Simon, the capitals of the framing colonnettes are of identical form. An exceptional base molding occurs in this relief, and also in the relief of Bartholomew. A more searching observation of the sculptures might perhaps enable one to determine an order of carving; but this would be complicated by the problem of deciding how many hands were at work and to what extent the variety is due, not to a development in time, but to different sculptors working together. The figure of Simon, I shall try to show later, was not carved by the same artist as the other apostles.[61] I have been unable to distinguish other hands on the piers since the variety is so considerable in small details, and the large effect so uniform. The sculptures were probably carved within a brief period in which development could hardly be considerable. Differences of design were varieties of the same conception or method; the progressing tendency toward more realistic art is inferred from details rather than the whole.

One may suppose that these details are sporadic deviations from a common type without any significance for future local styles. Yet their resemblance to a later more naturalistic art which maintains for a while the archaic conventions of the cloister permits us to assert that the style was not fixed and that the tendency of variation was toward the forms of later styles. It is conceivable that figures might grow more squat or their eyes more slanted; but the existence of five or six representations of ears which approximate in varying degree to the natural form makes it unlikely that the most natural was the first and that the cruder and deformed types were developed from it. Such a conclusion would run counter to the uniform technical skill of the reliefs; it would overlook also the association of the natural type with slightly later arts in which the forms show a corresponding character.

There are differences in the design of the figures which are even more difficult to interpret. It is enough to observe that this design already presents many of the features of subsequent Romanesque art, though the figures themselves are so flat and so much more schematically conceived than the works of the twelfth century.

The reliefs of each corner pier were not composed as separate slabs, but as intimately related pairs of figures. The apostles on the adjoining panels of the same pier face each other and sometimes reflect in their costumes, gestures, and linear schemes the artist's wish to accent an architectural unity. The pedestals and feet of the two apostles are identical; and on each pier some distinctive elements of dress or posture distinguish the two figures from those on the other piers.

The unity of the figures on one pier is itself archaic in that it is achieved by the duplication of forms. The complexity of their design is limited by the method of representation which admits only simple shapes, isolates the parts of an object as definite entities in the whole, and converts minor variations of a surface into ornamental markings.[62]

Fig. 18. Cloister; Pier Sculpture: St. Peter

This design, however, is already so asymmetrical and intricate and so nicely contrived, that the primitive conventions observed above constitute not the initial stages of an art, but a practiced archaism with a heritage of more realistic models from an unarchaic style. In several of the figures we note a less obvious ordering of details, unornamental combinations so arbitrarily accented that we can hardly doubt the deliberate aim. The sleeves of John form a continuous curve (Fig. 16) which is repeated in the long diagonal fold below. In the figure of James beside him (Fig. 15) the intricacy of the lines makes it difficult to distinguish the arbitrary or premeditated elements from the rhythmical character which emerges spontaneously in the execution of an artistic project. The arms, fingers, collar, mantle border, scroll, and feet form a series of rigorously coherent, but unobtrusively related diagonal lines, asymmetrical in scheme, unequally accented, and without the appearance of an imposed design. The incised curves of the mantle folds are subordinate to them. Horizontal lines of the suspended scroll repeat the steps of the pedestal, and several vertical folds and contours are emphasized in contrast and also as parallels to the columnar frame.

Neither the coherence nor intricacy of forms is a sufficient characterization of the design of these works. These qualities, like the peculiarities of representation isolated before, may be found in the arts of other times and places. The figures possess a distinctive Romanesque character which may be illustrated by analysis of several details.

Peter (Fig. 18) holds between his forefinger and the tip of his thumb two great keys which overlap slightly and then diverge. In accord with the conceptual process which governs the representation of forms in these reliefs, the two fingers are laid out flat in the same plane as the others, despite the physical impossibility of flexing the joints in this manner. In the same way, the circular handles of the keys are made to overlap so that each may be visible. The two keys are separated for the same reason, though the resulting relation of fingers and keys is strained and disturbing. This anatomically difficult gesture entails also an improbable twisting of the wrist.

Such distortion was not produced for clarity alone. On the contrary, the sculptor has enclosed these forms within a complicated whorl of concentric and radial lines, of which the two fingers and the rings of the keys appear to constitute the vortex.

The gestures add a note of animation and diagonal movement in the forms of the figures. The artistic effect of a single figure is obtained not only by the main contours and the larger folds of the garment, but by numerous curved lines, freely invented, inscribed on the surface of the body. These radiating lines are strongly contrasted; some folds have a wavy curvature, while others are in a forceful opposition to straight lines.[63]

This restless effect appears also in the contours of the figures. With all the elaboration of drapery lines the contours remain simple, but are nevertheless in accord with the patterning of the enclosed lines and limbs. They are asymmetrical, avoiding duplication of one side of the body by the other. They are formed by straight lines, with only occasional curves, and hardly suggest the flowing contours of the body. The normal attenuation of the waist and legs and the greater breadth of the shoulders are not observed. Even though these angular and harsh outlines are rarely modified by draperies which pass across the body, they are complicated by other means—by the jutting edges

Fig. 19. Cloister; Detail of Pier Sculpture: Head of St. James

Fig. 20. Cloister; Detail of Pier Sculpture: Head of Abbot Durand

of the mantle and the triangular bits of drapery that emerge from behind the figure (Figs. 15, 18, 21, 23, 27). There is produced in consequence a secondary contour which in its zigzag inequalities contrasts with the neighboring architectural frame. The interruption of the lower horizontal edge of the garments by the polygonal patterned folds described before contributes to the same end.

Even in the figure of Durand, who is represented with a deliberated precision, as if by compass and ruler, and whose neat, almost mechanical symmetry suggests an indifference to expression, the forms are not in ideal repose or clarity. The abbot is carved on the broadest of the nine reliefs, but his posture is extraordinarily strained. Standing like him, and enacting the same gestures, we would feel ourselves cramped, enclosed, and without firm support. The artist who reproduced with devotion the insignia of Durand's authority did not maintain in the smaller elements the ritual gravity inherent in the static architectural design of the whole. The details, though quite regular and schematic, break up the figure into numerous parts with contrasted axes.

At the very bottom are two vertical shoes of curved outline, bordered by a restless scalloped design, in contrast to the horizontal band of the ground. Then follows a series of overlapping surfaces, bounded by horizontal bands of unequal length. They include incised and sculptured perpendiculars, differently spaced on each surface, and so arranged that no continuity of verticals appears, but an endless interception of ornamental lines and overlapping of planes. The incised verticals (like the lower sides of the costume) tend toward the axis of the figure as they ascend; another triangle is implied in the relation of the two stoles to the small bit of the central band of the dalmatic visible below the tip of the orfrey. In contrast to the straight lines and perpendiculars of the alb, the tunic, and the stole, four triangular figures with curved hypotenuse are cut out symmetrically on the dalmatic by the descending chasuble.

The latter is dominated by a prominent vertical band enriched with jewels, forming the axis of the figure, like an everted spine. This orfrey divides the chasuble into two equal parts; their symmetry is sustained in the scrupulous correspondence of minor elements of the two sides. But these elements are so designed that the chasuble, viewed from top to bottom rather than from left to right, yields a perpetual contrast of lines and areas. Its lower boundary is ellipsoid, and recalls the shoes; its upper edge is a more complex form, with delicate ogee lines on the shoulders, rising to the ears and then returning to the chin in an opposed curve. Folds incised on the lower part of the chasuble form two sets of tangent asymmetrical loops, radiating from the orfrey like ribs from the spine. A more powerful contrast to the lower edge of the chasuble is provided by the rigid, diagonal jeweled bands, which meet near a point from which the loops descend.[64] The areas cut out on the breast between the orfrey, the shoulders, and the collar, with their elegant contrast of curves and straight lines, are typical of the whole in their restless angularity. Within these areas are incised other curves complementary to the loops of the lower chasuble, reversing their direction, and dividing the breast and shoulder into dissimilar but beautifully related areas. The subdivision of narrow angles, the radiation of these curves from the meeting point of contrasting diagonals, the interception of other lines which proceed to the same point (like the lower edges of the sleeves), and the groups of diagonal lines at the elbows—all these confer an additional restlessness on the central

Fig. 21. Cloister; Pier Sculpture: St. Bartholomew

Fig. 22. Cloister; Pier Sculpture: St. Matthew

portion of the figure. From this area of zigzag and diagonal movements we are brought back to a vertical-horizontal scheme by the erect arms, with simple folds perpendicular to the limbs. The surmounting hands resume the same scheme, but include the diagonal in an ingenious way. On the right hand the extended thumb parallels the sleeve and connects the architectural design of the hand with the sloping shoulder and with the diagonals and incised curves of the breast. Its direction is repeated by the other thumb, which bridges the crozier and the shoulder. This duplication is asymmetrical; but a more general symmetry is partly maintained by it. The force of the inward spiral curve of the crozier is countered by the outward turn of the thumb. The fingers are bent horizontally about the staff in another contrast to the same spiral curve. Analysis of the details of the hands and the crozier will reveal a most refined balancing of asymmetrical parts by inequality of interval, opposition of directions, and minute variations of relief.

The uppermost part of the figure, which is apparently simple and quite regular, includes the contrasts, encroachments, and interruptions of forms observed in the rest of the relief. This is clear in the banding of the collar with its overlapping folds and ornament and crescent shapes; in the halo which disappears under the arch and is broken by the spiral head of the crozier; and in the contrasts of the lines and surfaces of Durand's head, of the tonsured crown, the vertical hairs, the fillet, the arched eyebrows of double curvature, and the unusually long face, proportioned somewhat like the chasuble below.

I have tried to illustrate by this analysis of details a character of the whole. The reading of the separate parts in succession does violence to the simultaneous coherence of the object, but it enables us to follow the design of the work more easily, and to perceive in the complex adjustment of apparently simple parts their peculiarly involved and contrasted character in a whole which at first sight seems a bare archaic description.

A similar character may be found in the inscriptions of the piers. In the record of the consecration of the cloister (Fig. 24) the letters are closely packed, tangent to the frame and crossed or enclosed by each other. Even in the lower lines, which have larger letters, and where the artist could have spaced more broadly, he has preferred to crowd them, and to design them tangent to the frame. Where he is able to separate letters clearly he has chosen to accentuate their angularity and sharpness by triangular notches placed between them. The reason the border is

pinched inwardly at the angles and center of the lines may be found in the same character of the style. The artist could not accept two lines in clear unmodified parallelism; to animate the frame, to bring it nearer to the enclosed forms, he indented the border, anticipating Baroque frames.

The style may be grasped further by comparison of the Roman letters of the inscription with the corresponding classic forms. They are less regularly spaced, less uniformly proportioned than the latter; the verticals of letters like T, N, I, and L are not strictly parallel.[65] On the arches of the pier reliefs the sequence of letters is continually varied, and several different patterns are contrived from the inscriptions. The letter S is sometimes laid on its side.

The inscription of Durand's name and titles is even more obviously designed like the draperies of the figure. The spacing of the letters is rhythmical but irregular and complicated. The two Ns of DURANNUS are crossed in an exciting zigzag, and other letters intersect in monogram-like combinations. That the

Fig. 23. Cloister; Pier Sculpture: St. Philip

artist sought these effects and was not merely constrained by the narrowness of the surface and the length of the inscription is evident from the great variety in the amplitude of the letters, the irregularity of spacing of forms which in their individual details are cut with an obvious decisiveness, and from such peculiarities as the horizontal line passing through the BB of ABB(a)S, as a contraction of the word. Since it signified the omission of an A it might more plausibly have been placed above the second B and the S, instead of extending from the first A into the second B. The whole inscription is angular, crowded, intricate; the interruption of the text within a word (TOLOSANUS) at the crown of the arch distinguishes this Romanesque work from a classic inscription. Not only is an untextual element of religious character—a cross—introduced within a word, but the harmonious span of a curved line is thereby broken at its midpoint. We are reminded of the prominent keystones of Baroque arches, and of the aesthetic effect of the pointed construction.[66]

The design of the arcades of the galleries betrays an analogous conception (Fig. 8). The arches are not supported by a succession of uniform members, which we might expect from the uniformity of arches, but by columns alternately single and twin, and by occasional piers of prismatic form. This alternation lightens the arcade, diversifies the procession, introduces an element of recurrent contrast in what is otherwise a perfectly simple sequence, and makes of each bay an asymmetrical structure. For the arch springs on one side from a single capital and column, on the other from a twin combination; while in the adjoining bay this design is reversed. There results theoretically a larger symmetrical unit of two bays, bounded by single or twin columns; but this larger unit is not fixed and is hardly perceptible, since it is not embraced by a larger discharging arch or molding.[67]

I think it is apparent from this analysis that the intricacy and contrast of forms are not due merely to the survival of older complex elements in an archaic art; the latter is essentially devoted to such effects and produces them even in figures like the abbot Durand, whose costume and posture are significant mediaeval inventions. The symmetry of this relief is as fanciful as the less regular and traditional asymmetry of the apostles. Characteristics like the clear and generalized views of head, shoulders, and limbs, with their familiar archaic forms, are affected also by the dominant expressive bias of the style. Hence, perhaps, the retention of certain unarchaic features, like the remote eye of a profile head, and the frontal feet, suspended in a zigzag pattern.

It is also clear from the architectural context of the figures, their common material, their similarities in style, posture, frames, and ornament, that they are the product of a single enterprise and an already developed stable practice. The fact that in so restricted a project, under apparently uniform conditions of material and skill, variations of forms appear, with an unmistakable tendency toward more naturalistic and complex forms, is significant for the rapid development of western sculpture in the first half of the twelfth century. The variation is the more remarkable when we recall how stiff are the figures, how regular and formula-bound the representation of certain details.

Fig. 24. Cloister; West Gallery, Central Pier, Inscription of the Date of the consecration of the Cloister (1100)

Fig. 25. Cloister; Pier Sculpture: Head of St. Simon

THE CLOISTER CAPITALS

The arcades, which are reinforced at the ends and in the middle of each gallery by the piers of rectangular section, are supported by slender monolithic colonnettes, alternately single and twin (Fig. 8). On the east and west sides there are twenty arches, and on the others eighteen. The pointed arches are reconstructions of the thirteenth century, but spring from stone capitals, all of evident Romanesque origin. These capitals are seventy-six in number, alternately single and twin like the colonnettes which support

them. Those surmounting the corner colonnettes are engaged to the piers, and are cut in half vertically (Fig. 55). At one time two smaller arcades stood in the northwest corner of the cloister as enclosures of the fountain and the lavatorium of the monks.[68] They were of the same structure as the arcades of the galleries and were decorated like these by sculptured capitals. But the marble basin has disappeared, the arcades have been dismantled, the capitals scattered; and only the springing voussoirs of the arches which touched the gallery arcades have been left as traces of the original structure. Several colonnettes, as well as one capital and two impost blocks, are now preserved in the Belbèze collection in Moissac. They are of the same style as the capitals and imposts of the north gallery.[69]

Each capital, whether single or double, is composed of two parts, an inverted truncated pyramid and a rectangular impost block. Unlike classic art, the astragal is the base molding of the capital rather than the crown of the column. The capitals are with few exceptions circular in plan at the astragal, rectangular above at the impost. The transition from one form to the other is effected by an almost insensible flattening of the conical surface until the block assumes the section of a pyramid. (On several capitals the lower section is square or hexagonal, but the astragal remains circular.) By the salient relief of figures projecting from the ideal geometrical surface and by the structure of volutes and consoles, the change in section becomes imperceptible and the shape of the capital eludes a simple description.

The dimensions of the capitals vary according to their single or twin character; but in each class of capital they are nearly uniform. Exceptional dimen-

Fig. 26. Cloister; Detail of Pier Sculpture: Head of St. Andrew

Fig. 27. Cloister; Pier Sculpture: St. Simon

Fig. 28. Cloister; Detail of Pier Sculpture: Head of St. Paul

Fig. 29. Cloister; Detail of Pier Sculpture: Head of St. Peter

sions appear in the twin capitals of the west gallery (Fig. 32) which received also the arches of the destroyed lavatorium. Their broader bases are at once intelligible.[70]

In the design of the capitals it is difficult to discover a fixed system of proportions, since the initial blocks of the sculptor, probably quarried or rough-hewn in uniform dimensions, were trimmed unequally in the process of sculpture, and the original proportions altered. But several approximate ratios may be inferred from the measurements of the entire group, despite the occasional deviations. On the twin capitals the height of the drum is equal to the combined diameters of the two astragals (.30 to .32 plus); the upper breadth of the impost on its longer side is twice the height of the drum. This might be stated also: the diameter of the capital at the astragal is doubled in the height of the capital, quadrupled in the upper breadth of the impost. It is about equal to the height of the impost. The proportion of the heights of upper and lower impost bands is about that of the lower and upper breadth of a twin capital on its broader sides (.32: .50 and .065: .09, or .06: .10).

Of the visible surfaces of the impost—the upper, a horizontal band, and the lower, beveled—it is the second that receives the richer and more deeply carved ornament. The upper is covered with imbrications, in very low, almost shadowless relief, of many patterns; or is inscribed, or striped horizontally, or

given a decoration of flat lambrequins, triangles, lozenges, beads, arcatures, disks, and intersecting semicircles. These separate geometrical motifs are repeated in horizontal succession, tangent, or at regular intervals. On only a few imposts is a scheme of two alternating motifs employed, and these are usually very simple, like lozenge and bead, disk and dart, etc.

On the lower surface of the impost, however, a magnificent decoration of animal and plant forms is applied. Placed between the nonliving, geometric ornament of the upper surface and the human figures of the capital proper, it seems that, naively or by design, distinctions of vitality or importance have been rendered by distinctions of relief and of architecture. I shall not stop here to analyze this decoration, which deserves a separate study.

The drum of the capital retains several classic members. Two volutes form an upper frame of the figured scenes on each face. Usually they do not meet at the center but are interrupted by a triangle inscribed between them to form a zigzag. In the Miracle of Cana a central pair of volutes copies purer classical models (Figs. 30, 52). The central console block is likewise an ancient survival. Here its form is elaborated. No less than twelve different shapes may be counted, ranging from simple rectangular blocks, with one beveled surface, to finely curved consoles, not susceptible to an obvious geometrical description. The most elaborate and varied forms appear in the

Fig. 30. Cloister; Capital of East Gallery: Marriage at Cana

Fig. 31. Cloister; Capital at Corner of East Gallery: The Annunciation

south gallery, the simplest in the east. The astragals too receive different ornaments. The greater number are plain torus moldings, but several are cabled, and many have an ornament of lozengenets, ovals, imbrications, and horizontal strings, like the upper impost band. As on the consoles, the richest forms appear in the south gallery where astragal decorations are most common.

The surfaces of the capitals, below the volutes and consoles, are covered with human and animal figures or with foliate patterns. The latter are evident adaptations of the forms of the Corinthian capital; but on a few capitals palmettes rather than acanthus forms are employed, and the separate units are enclosed in scrolls in a manner unknown on the classic capital. The animals are mainly birds or lions confronted or adossed in simple heraldic groups. On several capitals human figures are placed between such animals or dragons. Stylistically, the animal and human forms on these capitals are not unlike those on the historiated ones. They are grouped somewhat more simply, but the anatomical structure, the contours, the modeling, the details of the features are quite similar to those of the narrative figures. Even the symmetrical grouping and the ornamental devices of these capitals recur in some of the religious compositions.

On the historiated capitals the figures are set on a neutral curved surface, in a relief which, though very low when measured in its absolute projection, is high in proportion to the size of the capitals and the figures. The scenes are spread out on all four faces of the capital; but we shall see that an effort was made to achieve pictorial unity by limiting separate incidents to a single face, and by framing the figures by the

Fig. 32. Cloister; Capital of West Gallery: Annunciation to the Shepherds

Fig. 33.
Cloister; Capital
of East Gallery:
The Three Span-
ish Saints, Au-
gurius,
Fructuosus, and
Eulogius

volutes and buildings carved at the angles. On several capitals of the east and west galleries (Figs. 30, 32, 33, 52, 67, 68, 75, 87) inscriptions are incised, sometimes with scattered letters, on the background surfaces between the figures. In the south and north galleries this practice is less common; it is only on the capitals of most primitive style that the background is treated in this way. On the more skillfully carved works the inscriptions are placed on the impost block or are incised on the capital itself in vertical and horizontal alignment. On no capitals of the cloister are the inscriptions more vagrant and decomposed than on those which show the greatest simplicity in the composition of the figures and a striving for symmetrical, decorative grouping of the episodes.

These inscriptions usually name the figures represented. Sometimes even the animals are accompanied by their names or initials (Fig. 32). On several capitals, not only the names of the actors but their actual speech is reproduced. On the capital of Cain and Abel, the Lord's question and Cain's reply are both incised on the common background. The abbreviated texts of the Beatitudes accompany the figures that personify these sentences (Fig. 82). Occasionally, as on the capitals narrating the miracle of St. Martin (Fig. 54) and the fall of Nebuchadnezzar (Fig. 47), whole lines from the illustrated text are copied on the imposts above the figures. The latter practice is a more refined device than the others. In the use of the inscriptions, as in the carving of the figures, may be observed various stages of archaism. The naming of the figures on the adjacent surface is a naive method known also in ancient art; the placing of a text above the scene is an advanced development.

* * * * *

When the sculptor of Moissac wished to represent the story of Adam and Eve he did not isolate a single incident from the Biblical text, but carved on the same surface the Temptation, the Lord's Reproach, the Expulsion, and the Earthly Labors of the pair. Adam appears four times in this one relief; we are asked to view the figures in a sequence in time as well as space, and to read them as we read the text they illustrate (Figs. 34, 39, 40).

The same primitive continuity of narrative appears

on most of the figured capitals of the cloister.

Since the entire surface of a capital could not be seen at one glance, it was admirably fitted for the continuous method of narrative sculpture. By limitation of the field visible at the same time, it escaped the inconsistency of several moments presented as simultaneous; in this respect it resembled the papyrus or parchment roll of ancient art and the columns of triumph on which successive scenes were deployed on a winding surface.

And like the ancient sculptors, who imposed a more complex dramatic unity on the separate incidents of the narrative sequence, the artists of Moissac practiced also those foreshortenings of episode which reveal the most action through the fewest gestures or figures. On the capital of the Martyrdom of John the Baptist, the martyr's head appears on the banquet table, while the figure of Salome at the right, with one hand raised, refers to another moment of the story (Fig. 2). The Expulsion of Adam and Eve likewise combines two incidents. On the south face the angel expels from Paradise two figures clad in the skins of beasts. Eve at the left grasps the branch of a tree projecting from the west face, where Adam reappears with a pruning tool. The Magi proceed from a building labeled Jerusalem and march to the Virgin and Child who are seated before Bethlehem; behind the first structure is enthroned Herod, ordering the

Massacre of the Innocents, which takes place before him. The scene is framed at the right by the same tower of Bethlehem (Figs. 35, 36, 37).

The continuous illustration of connected episodes in Moissac cannot be identified, however, with the classic or primitive process from which it differs in a peculiar manner. Whereas the continuity of representation on a column of triumph or a picture book like the Joshua Roll is maintained by a formal treatment which mingles the figures and backgrounds of successive episodes, so that the movement proceeds without interruption in a single direction, in Moissac four surfaces are demarcated on a capital and as many incidents are usually represented.[71] Here the continuous method is modified by the architectural isolation of scenes, further accented by the decorative unity of each surface. Each face of a capital is often bounded by single figures or buildings which frame the scene; the centralizing of action or design by the arrangement of elements about an apparent midpoint or axis confirms the discontinuity.

This difference from classical continuous illustration appears also in the variable and indeterminate direction of the story. Not only are scenes rendered as static symbolic arrangements or as architectural decorations, but incidents on adjacent sides of a capital may have no apparent connection.[72]

On the same capital the Magi approach the Virgin

Fig. 34. Cloister; Capital of East Gallery: Temptation of Adam and Eve

Fig. 35. Cloister; Capital of East Gallery: Journey of the Magi from Jerusalem; Herod Orders the Massacre of the Innocents

from the right (Fig. 36), while the Massacre of the Innocents proceeds from Herod seated at the left (Figs. 35, 37). The narrative order of the Adam and Eve capital is from right to left, of the Annunciation and Visitation, left to right (Figs. 31, 66); and in a scene like the Martyrdom of John (Fig. 2) the condensed narrative makes it difficult to judge whether the beheading at the right implies a movement from right to left or the reverse.[73] Without indication of an end or starting point there cannot be a legible order or direction in scenes placed on the four sides of a pyramid. In the Temptation of Christ (Figs. 38, 84) each of the four incidents is isolated; and by no possible interpretation of gestures can we infer the textual order of the incidents. The feeding of Christ by the angels, which terminates the action in the Gospels, is in fact placed here between the second and third temptations (Fig. 38).

Each scene is usually so self-contained in composition that only before a few capitals, which will be considered later, have we an impulse to shift our position the better to grasp the sense or structure of a group.

Even when two incidents appear upon the same face of a capital they are so designed that a single decorative composition emerges; the two actions di-

verge from a common axis (Figs. 35, 96). This is not the succession of movements characteristic of continuous illustration.

This peculiarity of the narrative method in Moissac is an essential feature of the style; hence the analysis of its elements and the distinction from other types of continuous illustration are instructive.

It seems to be occasioned by the architecture of the capital, which is crowned by a rectangular member. The impost commands a separate attention to the figures under each of its sides, and these are consequently treated as closed fields.

Such an explanation is incomplete, however. The rectangularity of the impost was itself designed by the sculptor; its clear, sharply defined surfaces, its geometric ornament in low relief, indicate to us that the shape of the impost was not an anterior condition that determined the grouping of the figures but was conceived as an element of the whole like the figures themselves, and shared with them a common archaic character.

The pointed arches and ornament of Gothic picture frames will clarify this relation. The irregular forms within the pictures are not determined by these boundaries; both are specifically Gothic creations. The analogy of frame and enclosed forms (as in the

Romanesque works) is a common mediaeval feature.

The compact grouping of figures under a single side of an impost is not merely meant to define limits of action or space; it is also decorative and approaches in the pervasiveness of its often symmetrical design the quality of pure ornament. The trapezoidal shape of the surface, with the broader side above, like a blazon, contributes to its heraldic effect. A scene has thus a double aspect: it is a religious illustration, and like the foliate and animal ornament of other capitals it is an abstract architectural design. Even the most literal representations have this decorative character; the formal distinction between narrative illustration and decoration is inapplicable here, though some capitals with fewer figures have a more obvious ornamental design than others.

In the early Romanesque ornament of Moissac the

motif is designed as an ideal example of the simplest and most general relations evident in the actual object represented. The petals of a flower are strictly assimilated to a radial structure, and the repetition of the flower itself constitutes a regular series of which the elements are equivalent. The more complex details are submitted to a similar process. The curling of the petals is uniform in relief and may be defined in geometrical terms. The asymmetrical plant forms in scrolls are no less regular. Their unequal lobes constitute an ideal helicoid pattern.

In the same way the grouping of figures in religious themes often reproduces the most general relations of objects. Figures with the same function are often parallel and similar in gesture. The simplicity of the shapes of the figures is maintained in their combinations.

But this archaic rendering of narrative or drama is only one factor in the decorative character of the whole. Besides this conceptual simplicity there is the apparent assimilation of the objects to the architecture of the capital and the style of ornament. The architecture of the capital is not an external element which imposes itself on the illustration and determines its form, but, as I remarked of the impost, it is itself a conception analogous to the ornament and the figures. It has a similar archaism and a similar expressiveness. Its pronounced diagonals, its symmetry, its accented contrast of surfaces, its centralized zigzag frame and volutes, all these are correlates of the figure style.

The inverted trapezoidal field of each side of the capital demanded either distortion and seeming instability of corner figures or ingenious accommodations. The sculptor sacrificed plausibility to decoration. In the capital of Adam and Eve the edicule representing the gate of Paradise is inclined at an angle more precarious than that of any leaning tower.[74] The figure of Eve at the other end also follows the sloping profile of the capital; and on the north face, the Lord and the tree are composed diagonally (Fig. 40). This is true of most of the figures and objects placed under the volutes of the cloister capitals. Regarded from the side, these figures appear vertical and stable; but the rest of the capital is thereby distorted. It is obvious that the sculptor usually planned the capital as a series of four separate surfaces, and adapted the composition to the trapezoidal shape (regardless of a probably unacknowledged conflict with natural appearances) while exploring its decorative and expressive possibilities.

The sculptural field is bounded not only by the diagonal sides of the inverted trapezoid, but by an even more unusual upper frame. For the figures must be fitted under the zigzag formed by the volute bands and a triangle of which the apex touches the central console. This upper frame appears on all four sides of most of the capitals. It is a survival of the Corinthian capital and illustrates the preservation of no longer relevant parts of a parent form even when the artistic

Fig. 39.
Cloister; Capital
of East Gallery:
Expulsion of
Adam and Eve

Fig. 40.
Moissac,
Cloister; Capital
of East Gallery:
Adam before the
Lord

Fig. 41.
Cloister; Capital
of North Gal-
lery: Miracle of
St. Benedict

31

character of the offspring is altogether different from its ancestor's. The central triangle is a flattened angularized version of the central leaf of the upper row of acanthus of a rough-hewn Corinthian capital. In the capitals of the Three Hebrews (Fig. 95), St. Benedict (Figs. 41, 42), St. Martin (Fig. 54), and the Crusaders before Jerusalem (Fig. 49), the original leaf appears between the volute bands with its curved tip and axial ridge. There is reason to believe that this was not an unnoticed survival or merely traditional routine. For on the capitals representing Adam and Eve and the Martyrdom of St. Laurence (Figs. 57, 96), the central console is modeled in the form of a rough-hewn acanthus leaf. And in the Wedding of Cana (Fig. 30), where the usual triangle is absent, it is replaced by a pair of central volutes as in the true Corinthian capital. The free use of the volutes, the simplified curved leaf form and its flattened triangular derivative as equivalent motifs on the same part of the capital, shows that the sculptors were aware of their original structural sense, and that whoever employed the triangle knew of its more plastic source. Where neither leaf, nor triangle, nor central volutes appear (Annunciation to Shepherds, Fig. 32; St. Saturninus, Fig. 43) their place is always occupied by a central object—a head, tower, or plant form—so that the symmetry of the upper frame and of the capital as a whole is not disturbed.

The zigzag frame is not an ordinary diagonal motif or a regular zigzag. The greater breadth of the two outer lines, the variety of angles, the distinction of an inner triangle, the termination by spiral volutes—all these constitute a symmetrical centralized structure, unlike the endless zigzag of pure ornament.

On the broader surfaces of the twin capitals the central triangle of the upper frame has an evident similarity to the junction of the lower parts. At this junction there is usually a triangular concavity. The zigzag frame provides also a transition from the sloping sides of the capital to the diagonal profile of the beveled band of the impost. It gives a greater elegance to the form of the capital by its vertical and diagonal directions and spiral endings. As a restless angular form crowning figures in action this frame participates in the expression of the sculptured forms and confirms a quality of the design already observed in the piers. Like the sloping sides of the capital it precludes a classic tectonic structure in the composition. Set in this architecture of the capital, the figure is tilted, not vertical and horizontal.

* * * * *

Where the subject provided only two or three figures, or suggested a central theme and two equal accessories, the artist was frankly decorative. In the Annunciation to the Shepherds (left of Fig. 32), the two goats confronting the central plant hardly seem part of a narrative theme, and are indistinguishable in design from the purely ornamental animal figures. It is true that this face of the capital has been inscribed to suggest a relation to the story; but even the inscription is an ornament, and is arranged symmetrically. The word "cabras" is incised behind each goat, and on the right side is written backwards, with the letters reversed, ⱯᴚᙠⱯƆ. This is not illiteracy, as has been supposed, but the result of an artistic intention.[75] On

Fig. 42. Cloister; Capital of North Gallery: Miracle of St. Benedict— Monk Tempted by Demon

Fig. 43. Cloister; Capital of East Gallery: Martyrdom of St. Saturninus— the Accusation of the Saint

the central console block another inscription (SISVA—for SILVA) designates a palm between the goats as a forest. On the adjoining face of the same capital, a similar heraldic design represents Daniel between the lions (Fig. 86). Here too, the rampant animals are adossed, heads turned to each other, next to the central seated prophet with symmetrically orant hands. The inscriptions are likewise distributed in

parallel ornamental schemes. As in textile patterns, the interspaces between the figures are filled, though here with letters.[76]

Even on capitals without such animals the artist has contrived human figures as schematically grouped as the animals in ornamental combinations. On a capital like the Adoration of the Cross a symmetrical arrangement was inevitable; two angels stand beside a

Fig. 44.
Cloister; Capital
of West Gallery:
Angel

33

central cross. But on the east and west faces of the same capital an isolated figure of an angel has been more arbitrarily bent to a decorative pattern from which results an angelic radiance (Fig. 44). He stands with outstretched arms in the center of the field between the great wings of the adjoining angels of the other sides of the capital. His own wings are spread out in diagonal lines repeating the volutes of the frame; his mantle forms a semicircle in contrast to these straight lines, and repeats the curves of the wings of the adjoining angels. The legs of these figures constitute a powerful diagonal frame below, while minor curves of drapery on the central figure repeat and diffuse these tangent arcs throughout his body.

This axial mass is not a rigid center of the theme, but is itself twisted and turned to produce within the heart of the design an energetic asymmetry, which includes the circular movements of the larger outer forms. The head is turned to the right, the feet to the left; the diagonal of the torso is opposed to that of the left leg, so that a zigzag results from the movements of the limbs, which is accented by the jeweled band across the breast and the diagonal edge of the tunic across the legs. An additional contrast is produced by the asymmetrical nimbus. The whole figure is cast in a stiff *contrapposto*, in which we can detect, however, a symmetrical organization from top to bottom in the contrasted directions of the head and feet, the torso and legs.

In the east gallery, on the capital of the Martyrdom of Peter and Paul, an angel carries the nude souls of the two saints in his arms (Fig. 45). He stands in the very middle of the field, his head and halo on the central console, his wings outstretched to form a background of the relief and a frame. The little figures are identical in gesture and position; their arms diverge in loops from the angel's breast as his wings

spread out from behind his head. The legs of the martyrs emerge from a widening pit, wedged in the narrow base of the field between the sides of the triangular frame.

The souls of the three Spanish martyrs (Fig. 77) are similarly grouped. They are enclosed, standing and orant, in one mandorla, between two angels. The hand of God appears on the console on the upper point of the jeweled glory.[77]

Such a centralized design occurs also in the Martyrdom of St. Saturninus (Fig. 46). In the scenes from the life of St. Martin the figure of Christ holds the divided mantle between two angels. In these works the marked symmetry is not merely a conventional device of composition; it penetrates the smaller elements of design, and controls gestures, contours, and accessories to such a degree that the whole may be analyzed with ease.

In the hagiographic scenes, especially, the formalizing of gesture, composition, and small details of drapery, so that the whole appears prearranged, permanent, and hierarchic, has an air of liturgical seriousness. Here the order implied in symmetry has religious as well as artistic significance.

This centralized design is also apparent in the architectural representations. Where a building occupies the face of a capital it is placed in the middle and flanked by towers or other paired structures. Sometimes the building is a narrow tower in the middle of the field, separating two groups of figures that are usually disposed parallel to each other in gesture or movement (Figs. 35, 96).

In the examples of symmetrical composition cited above, the subject is essentially static and implies no dominant movement across the surface of the capital. There are other capitals in which episodes rather than symbols or hieratic groups have been submitted to a similar conception. In the representation of the

Fig. 45. Cloister; Capital of East Gallery: Angel with Souls of Peter and Paul

Fig. 46. Cloister; Capital of East Gallery: The Soul of St. Saturninus in Glory

Fig. 47. Cloister; Capital of South Gallery: Daniel Interpreting the Dream of Nebuchadnezzar

wise man (possibly Daniel) interpreting the dream of Nebuchadnezzar (Fig. 47), the central position of the king is not merely official; it is an iconographic correlate of a design in which the symmetry has been maintained by numerous accessories. The three figures are framed by three arches; the axis is confirmed in the arched contour of the console; and the king sits with legs crossed symmetrically in the very middle of the field.

On the capital of the Martyrdom of Stephen, the saint preaching to the Jews is placed in the center of the surface on a seat with diagonal legs which repeat

the triangle above his halo (Fig. 92). The trefoil edge of the console is a further means of centralizing the action. Two figures who menace the saint stand at his sides with arms raised in similar diagonal gestures. Also, in the adjoining scene of Stephen led by his accusers, he stands in the center of the field (Fig. 48); if he faces the right, the symmetry of the whole is maintained by the flanking figures, who are slightly differentiated to balance the inequality produced by the direction of Stephen's movement. How intently the sculptor was preoccupied with closed compositions of clear and finely sustained symmetry we may

Fig. 48. Cloister; Capital of South Gallery: Arrest of Stephen

35

see in the arbitrary extension of Stephen's mantle, flying to the left and forming a diagonal mass and a movement which correspond to the extended arm on the other side.

In the Massacre of the Innocents (Fig. 37) two mothers with infants in their arms are placed in the middle of the field and are so designed with their children that they constitute a perfectly symmetrical group. This conception is all the more significant for the primacy of a decorative end in representation because the symmetry is maintained at the sides of this group by two soldiers who belong to different moments of the action. The soldier at the left faces Herod, who is seated on the western surface of the capital and commands him to massacre the children: The soldier at the right faces the eastern side of the capital on which are superposed the murdered children and their detached limbs. Elements of three actions are combined in a single centralized static group.

The crusaders before Jerusalem (Fig. 49) are not represented in procession, but are grouped in twos in symmetrical adaptation to the field. Each bears a great spear or axe in his extended arm, parallel to the diagonal edge of the capital.

In the scene of the Calling of the Apostles, Christ stands between the waves with arms extended symmetrically; his arms and shoulders parallel the zigzag frame of the capital, while groups of fishes, arbitrarily introduced beside him, form a lower diagonal frame (Fig. 50). In the adjoining scenes of the fishermen

almost every detail has been subjected to a preconceived symmetry (Fig. 51). The waves despite their continuity are made to diverge from the center of the capital like two undulating wings; the net is suspended from the exact midpoint of the boat; and two volutes spring from within the boat to meet directly beneath the central console. The symmetry is beautifully sustained by the clear and uniform succession of relief surfaces. I feel that the trefoil section of the console (Fig. 51) was thoughtfully designed so that the entire scene might culminate in a symmetrical object with a salient central mass between analogous forms in lower relief. Its convexity provides a necessary contrast to the concave center of the lower portion of the field.

The subordination of narrative to architectural design is apparent in a remarkable detail of the Adoration of the Magi (Fig. 36). Two great petaled flowers are carved on the volute bands near the spiral ends. They are symmetrically placed and seem a purely ornamental addition to the theme. But an inscription next to each flower tells us that they are stars; they are labeled OR to designate the eastern star followed by the wise men. The repetition of the star can only illustrate its double appearance to the men, and its movement before them as they marched to Bethlehem. ("And, lo, the star which they saw in the east, went before them, till it came and stood over where the young child was." Matthew, ii, 9.) The textual recurrence in time has been converted into a static ornament, and even the star itself has become a

Fig. 49. Cloister; Capital of North Gallery: The Crusaders

Fig. 50. Cloister; Capital of North Gallery: The Calling of the Apostles—Christ

flower.

But not all the capitals are composed so obviously. There are some which are regular in grouping, but a prominent central theme is avoided. The Miracle of Cana (Fig. 52) is in this respect most remarkable and subtle. In the middle of the field is the hand of Christ, hardly apparent, bearing a short horizontal magic stick; under it, the three jars of water, symmetrically grouped, and above it, an open symmetrical book held out by the apostle to the left. Above the book are two immense central tangent volutes in high relief, like the corresponding jars below and the heads of the figures. The volutes are crowned by five tonguelike processes, arranged to parallel the three jars and the two adjoining figures. The diagonal bands of the central volutes form the sides of an equilateral triangle of which the base is the horizontal molding behind the jars. Together they invert the shape of the whole capital and frame the miraculous symbolic center theme. The edges of the mantles of Christ and the opposite apostle prolong the volute diagonal to the bottom of the capital, while above, the haloes and the outer volute spirals carry the central volute motif across the upper part of the capital.[78] Further observation of this mutilated relief will reveal more correspondences of line, spacing, and mass that confirm our initial impression of the orderliness of its structure and its perfection of simple rhythmical form.

In the wedding scene on the same capital (Fig. 30) the figures are aligned in obvious succession, but monotony is avoided by a division into two groups, sepa-

Fig. 51. Cloister; Capital of North Gallery: The Calling of the Apostles— the Apostles Fishing

rated only at the upper and lower frame by pairs of central volutes, and by the variation of parts like the hands, the feet, and the dishes. A fine touch is the extension of the table before only five figures; the sixth stands at the right and is the only diner whose entire figure is visible. A further asymmetry is created by the intrusion of the bride's tunic among the equal feet, ranged under the table like so many architectural supports.

Although the table seems to extend across the whole capital its center is not on the axis, but to the left, under the third figure (from the left) who encroaches more upon the table than any of the other diners. If the symmetry of the whole is modified by this isolation of five figures within the large series, the outer four of these, in turn, are placed symmetrically beside the third figure. The four diners at the ends of the table are disposed in equal groups of two by their common gestures and occupation with the food, and by the parallel incised folds of the tablecloth. The position of the bread on the table, in the middle of the capital rather than of the table, and the grouping of the feet below (as well as of the heads and volutes) assure the dominance of the main symmetry of six figures rather than of the five. But the symmetry of the latter is an effective disguise which gives a movement and variety to a simple, regular series without disturbing either its symmetry or its effect of casual, unforced placing. It is interesting to observe how unique is each figure, how different the amplitude of the separate masses, and the overlapping of bodies, arms, and hands.

In the Adoration of the Magi the sculptor's problem was to relate an enthroned Virgin and Child to

Fig. 52.
Cloister; Capital
of East Gallery:
Miracle of Cana

three Magi in procession (Fig. 36). Although he followed the "Hellenistic" tradition which placed the sacred group at one end, he preserved the monumental frontality of ancient Eastern prototypes in setting the Virgin and Christ under the left volute unattentive to the three kings.

The composition is so simple and unpretentious that its solution of the problem will appear only on close scrutiny. The sculptor has managed to wrest a symmetrical scheme from an apparently unsusceptible subject by dividing the four units (the Virgin and Christ are one) into two groups, each set in one of the halves of the twin capital. He has made the first Magus, who adjoins the Virgin, smaller than his fellows. The two stars, already mentioned, are placed symmetrically on the volute bands above the figures. Lest the sharp line between the two halves of the

capital be too striking a division, it is crossed by the salient mantle end of the second Magus. The garments of all three are thus blown forward, forming jutting triangles. With the raised arms of the Magi, carrying gifts, and the advancing legs, this mantle edge participates in a strong vertical zigzag movement, parallel in the three figures and opposed to their horizontal procession. By this means the predominantly vertical and triangular character of the Virgin theme is brought into relation with the horizontal order of the other three units. The flying drapery above her head is in this respect also significant.

Groupings of an asymmetrical or uncentralized character are not uncommon in the cloister. Although the presence of unlike objects in the story—man and beast, figures standing, seated, and recumbent, or characters in subordinate relation—does not

Fig. 53. Cloister; Capital of East Gallery: St. Saturninus Dragged by the Bull

Fig. 54.
Cloister; Capital
of North Gal-
lery: St. Martin
Dividing his
Mantle

conflict with and even suggests an ornamental grouping in some works (Daniel, Shepherds and Goats,
Crucifixion of Peter, etc.), the subject could not be
bent to such a scheme, or would not be treated in this
manner, by an artist of more complex style. This is
especially true of the work of the sculptor of the south
gallery. In his capitals the more complicated asymmetrical conceptions sometimes include an approximate symmetry. Even among the more archaic capitals, beside the striving for symmetry and regular
alignment, less schematic structures appear. But they
are usually more compact, massive, and enclosed
than those of the south gallery capitals and display
simpler lines and rhythms. We have seen in the Miracle of Cana how the sculptor has modified the general
symmetrical design in varying the equality of parts
and the smaller details of drapery, gesture, and
accessories.

On the capital of the Anointing of David (Fig. 85)
the gestures of the figures, the horn of Samuel, and
the mantle of David have been disposed to form sim-

ple curves, with a clear rhythmical alternation of concave and convex lines, as in arabesque patterns. The
turn of the horn has an obvious relation to the arbitrarily extended and curved mantle of David. That
this arrangement was deliberate seems evident from
an unusual asymmetry in the framing volute bands:
the central triangle, above David's head, is irregular
in uniting the curve of the horn with the left volute.
The contours of the figures are so simple that the
ideal geometrical framework of the relief coincides
with forms of the figures, as in the capitals with foliate
ornament.

On this capital the curvilinear scheme, which has
also an illustrative value, producing an intense and
active union of the two figures corresponding to the
episode, is concentrated in the center of the field. A
related design is sometimes spread across an entire
surface. We see this in the figure of the apocalyptic
dragon in the south gallery and in the scenes from the
lives of Benedict and Martin in the north. In the
latter, Martin and the horse together are a prepon-

derant mass (Fig. 54); the beggar is in posture and form so unlike the saint and the horse that the unity of the relief appears all the more remarkable. The sculptor has connected the two figures by a series of curves extending across the upper half of the field— curves formed by the great wing of an angel brought over from an adjoining face, by the raised arms of Martin and the beggar, and by the concentric loops of the garment held between them. Related curves are abstracted from the beggar's ribs and skirt and from the body of the horse.

Even in the ordinarily asymmetrical theme of the Sacrifice of Isaac (Fig. 55) the sculptor has centralized the figure of the boy. If the whole is not strictly symmetrical, it is organized with respect to a symmetrical zigzag and diagonal frame. But unlike the Anointing of David the whole is decidedly angular, with many sharp oppositions which transmit the quality of the episode itself. An angel behind Isaac corresponds to the figure of Abraham; the contours of his zigzag wings resemble the volute bands, the central triangle, and the gestures and knife of the patriarch. Isaac sits

on a triangular heap of stones, and his own body is a structure of diagonal lines.

On the capital of the Deliverance of Peter (Fig. 81) three men with great pointed shields stand under the polylobed Moorish archway that symbolizes the prison. The symmetry here is inevitable; but the angel and Peter on the adjoining face lend themselves less readily to such repetition. Whereas Peter is chained and bent, the angel soars down from the clouds under the volute, almost horizontally extended. In the beautiful design of his outspread wings, the halo, and the movement of head and arms, he forms a linear sequence opposing, diffusing, and repeating the contours of Peter below. The curves of both figures are contrasted with similar straight diagonals of towers and walls and the volutes of the capital itself. The relief of the figures and the buildings also participates actively in the design. Nowhere else in the cloister is the surface of a capital so completely covered by as varied lines and planes, or is the play of forms so concentrated and rich. The building of the adjacent side of the capital encroaches upon this side.

Fig. 55. Cloister; Capital of West Gallery: Sacrifice of Isaac

Fig. 56.
Cloister; Capital
of South Gal-
lery: The Vision
of John

Its corner is not under the volute but so far within the scene of Peter and the angel that it connects the former's foot with the angel's sleeve, and marks the meeting of two plane surfaces that break up the ordinary neutrality of the background and contrast with the rounded forms of the two figures.

In the Appearance of the Angel to John, also in the south gallery (Fig. 56), we see a similar rhythmic grouping of two asymmetrically superposed figures.

John reclines on an unsupported bed suspended on the wall; the angel, emerging as before from under the volute, grasps his arms. The rear wing of the angel is carried across the capital to the other volute. Examining the upper contour of this figure we discover that it is a continuous line of disguised symmetrical character. Its highest point is the angel's head beneath the console, from each side of which extend wing forms of subtly varied contour prolonged to the volute spirals. Likewise below, the arms of the angel are nicely duplicated by the pleated folds of his hanging mantle on the right; and the opposed left arm of John finds its symmetrical counterpart in a diagonal molding along the outer edge of the same mantle. In this scene the apparent network of intricate, freely rhythmical shapes includes a larger though not instantly apparent, symmetrical structure. The grouping of the heads and arms of the two figures, if regarded with respect to a diagonal axis, will reveal itself as a simple scheme of two equal opposed heads separated by a triangle of which the base is formed by their united outer arms, and the sides by the opposed inner ones. As a completing touch (which helps establish the symmetry of the scene) this triangle is crowned by another of which the apex is the left volute; the sides are the angel's wing and the diagonal wall of John's chamber (only barely visible in the photograph). The sculptor has won a symmetrical disposition from the whole group by the extension of the angel's wings, the centralizing of his head, the incision in low relief of two side walls rising to the volutes, and by the prolongation of John's coverlet to form a simple base. Where the story contradicted this regularity of design, as in the opposition of the two figures, he has shaped the resistant elements into another symmetrical group, but with respect to a diagonal axis parallel to the inclination of their heads and the left volute band. To unite these three systems of horizontal, vertical, and diagonal axes he has multiplied certain folds and extended the wings so that a harmonious interpenetration results. Thus the volute

bands are prolonged in the distorted right arm of the angel and the falling mantle-edge, while, in the space between, trapezoids and triangles are inscribed to duplicate the structure of the capital and to link objects more intensely than is possible by gesture alone.[79]

In the east gallery, on a capital of which some actors are aligned in simple repetition—the Washing of the Feet—the figures of different pose share in a beautiful play of line and of the masses of body and limbs (Fig. 75). The first impression of the utter awkwardness and lack of skill of this sculptor, produced by the squatness of the apostles, their thick folds and homely bodies, yields to a perception of the nicety of his feeling for linear rhythm and massing. As in the Vision of John, the work of a far more skilled sculptor, the diagonals of the joined arms of Christ and Peter intervene between the heads, and the contours of the bodies bring apparently casual movements into intimate plastic relation.

It would take too long to inquire into the structure of each scene in the cloister. Those analyzed above have been summarized rather than read thoroughly. And no two capitals are identical in design. The symmetry is of variable shapes and combinations, while within the skeleton of axial structure are developed less simple but as rhythmical articulations.

I have considered so far mainly those scenes which form closed compositions corresponding to a single trapezoidal field of a capital. In several sculptures a scene is not isolated by means of figures or objects placed at the sides of the field, and the action is expanded across two or three faces of the capital. But

Fig. 57.
Cloister; Capital of East Gallery: St. Laurence on the Grill

Fig. 58.
Cloister; Capital of South Gallery: The Chaining of the Devil

even in such works the single surfaces retain their compositional unity; the figures are so contrived that if each face of the capital were isolated and the figures cut off at the ideal frame of the trapezoid, the resulting design would be balanced and complete, despite the incompleteness of illustration.[80]

In the Martyrdom of Laurence the angels who cense and fan the body of the saint, lying on the central grill (Fig. 57), extend in symmetrical correspondence across the upper part of the capital. Their wings correspond too and help frame the scene; but the bodies of the angels actually emerge from the volutes of the adjoining faces. In the same way the symmetrical bellows beside the grill are held by executioners represented on adjacent sides of the capital.

On the capital of the Three Hebrews in the Fiery Furnace (Fig. 95) the action, extending around the entire capital, forms separate structures as symmetrical and decorative as the most rigorously designed aal ornaments. The Hebrews stand in the *corners* under the volutes, with arms outstretched—one arm on each side of the capital. The center of the field is occupied by flames—symmetrical wavy processes, like gigantic vegetation. The orant arms of the Hebrews parallel the waves and complete the orna-

ment of flames. But these arms, considered from the corner of the capital, form a symmetrical enclosure of the figure and a zigzag movement in contrast to the volutes. Even the costumes of the figures reflect this conception in the zigzag ends of the tunics, a reminiscence of Oriental costume traditional in this scene. When we regard the figures in relation to the frame we understand why the Hebrews were not placed in the center of the field under the consoles.

In these two works the unenclosed narrative was easily submitted to symmetrical designs. But in some subjects the action has a dominant direction which could not be bent to so formalized an arrangement. On a capital of the south gallery, devoted to the apocalyptic Chaining of the Dragon (Fig. 58), the monster is led by an angel who emerges from under the volute of one side and extends across the adjacent surface of the capital, up to a building which occupies its far end. That the single surfaces were considered as compositional units, despite the obvious direction and continuity of the scene, is apparent from the position of the dragon who occupies almost the whole of one field, and from the extension of the garment and wings of the angel to complete the design of a field in which he himself does not participate. By this extension the unity of episode is furthered, insofar as the angel who is turned away from the dragon is thereby connected with him. It is possible that the illustrative significance affected the design, for the dragon is placed asymmetrically in the field to admit this extension of wings and clothing, and his tail is coiled upward to form a mass corresponding to these parts of the angel and a movement parallel to them. Despite the asymmetry of the beast he is placed so that his prominent bulk occupies the center of the field; in the correspondences of the angel and the monster's

Fig. 59. Cloister; Capital of South Gallery: The Good Samaritan Pays the Innkeeper

Fig. 60. Cloister; Capital of South Gallery: Descent from the Mountain

tail there is an evident symmetry. Even within the latter's body an analogous correspondence has been contrived in the assimilation of his large head and the lower wing.

The conception of the surfaces of the capital as isolated fields with enclosed designs seems to be contradicted by such expanded episodic themes as the Good Samaritan (Fig. 59) and the Transfiguration (Figs. 60, 88). In the latter the conception differs from the traditional type in that the three apostles are grouped on one side of Christ, the two prophets on the other. The rare theme of the Descent from the Mountain is also represented (Fig. 60). In the first scene the three apostles, who are placed on two sides of the capital, move in one direction. By dividing them so that two are on the south face and the third is on the east next to Christ, the sculptor was able to

enclose each face of the capital and yet retain the effect of a narrative composition with a single marked direction. On the south face a palm tree placed under the volute arrests the forward movement of the two apostles; while a third figure at the other end of the same face, belonging to another scene (the Descent from the Mountain) and moving in the opposite direction, balances the first group. We see on this side of the capital elements of two distinct episodes combined without intelligible relation, yet perfectly coordinated as relief compositions. Here the archaic clarity pertains less to meanings than to forms.

If the figure of Christ in the Transfiguration is not isolated between the two prophets, as in the imposing traditional images of the subject, he retains, nevertheless, a central position between one apostle and one prophet. The second prophet, under the volute,

Fig. 61. Cloister; Capital of South Gallery: The Vision of John—Apocalyptic Rider

45

is balanced by the palm tree already described. Christ faces the right, like the apostle beside him; but this strong direction is countered by the opposite movement of the prophets and the vigorous diagonal extension of the arm of the first prophet.

Even in the Descent from the Mountain (Fig. 60), in which four figures proceed in the same direction, the sculptor has cast the whole group into a balanced pattern. One apostle has been placed in the exact center of the field under the console; on one side he is flanked by Christ and a building (the tabernacles of Peter), on the other by two apostles. If they all walk toward the left, the upper body of Christ is turned back to regard the apostles, and two figures make gestures of the hand opposed to the direction of their march.

It is in the same spirit that this sculptor, in the beautiful figure of the Apocalyptic rider (Fig. 61), has opposed the lion's movement by the angel's flying mantle and the extended wing behind him to form a closed composition.

It is apparent, too, that in capitals of the south gallery and in several of the north the composition of single faces is not so deliberately enclosed as on the other capitals; the horizontal direction of narrative is more pronounced even if finally submitted to a balanced scheme. The corner figures or objects sometimes participate in two actions on these capitals. In the Healing of the Centurion's Servant, Christ stands under the volute; his body is turned toward the figures on one side of the capital, his head toward the centurion on the other (Fig. 62).

This obvious continuity of action is not, as one might suppose, a more primitive stage of representation, a sort of pictographic procession of elements. On the contrary, the rendering of action in these capitals is more subtle and complicated than in the

firmly enclosed static groups. In the latter, the figures usually maintain a single direction in their gestures and bodily movement. When such figures confront each other, they are often completely determined by this relation, while in the south gallery a figure points in one direction and looks in another.[81] In conversation he may indicate the subject or reference by an equivocal posture which symbolizes his attention to two objects. The centurion imploring Christ points at the same time to his servant who lies in bed behind him (Fig. 62); and Christ, as I have already observed, has an analogous complexity of gesture. The whole body is animated by a contrast of movements which in its repeated and uniform application recalls the mannered *contrapposto* of the sixteenth century as well as the later Romanesque style of southern France.

That the narrative composition described above is a more complex type than the first, and yet distinct from the simple narrative continuity of the more primitive arts, is confirmed by the striking tendency toward asymmetrical composition in the capitals of the south gallery. The symmetrical elements of such scenes as the Angel appearing to John (Fig. 56) are hardly as explicit as in the capitals of martyrdom. Even in themes inherently suited to a symmetrical form the sculptor has willfully diverted certain elements to create a more intricate balance than was ordinarily attained in the cloister.

On the capital of the Four Symbols of the Evangelists (Fig. 63) the human figure lends himself readily to a central position under the console block. The head is inscribed in the usual triangle between the volutes, and the disproportionately great wings are extended to fill the surface. The opened book in his hands is placed at the very center of his torso, marking the axis of the body. But the garment of the lower body is blown by the wind and extends unequally

Fig. 62.
Cloister; Capital of South Gallery: Christ and the Centurion of Caphernaum

Fig. 63.
Cloister; Capital of South Gallery: Symbols of the Evangelists— the Man of Matthew

Fig. 64.
Cloister; Capital of South Gallery: Symbols of the Evangelists— the Eagle of John

46

across his legs, so that the right contour has a marked triangular salience, while the left is an unbroken line. This disturbance of the equality of two parts similar in function and shape in a scheme otherwise rigidly symmetrical has an obvious motivation. On another side of the same capital (Fig. 64) the eagle is carved in profile rather than in the heraldic frontality we might expect. This is one of the finest conceptions in Romanesque art; it is at the same time monumentally grand and delicate. The nimbed head set under the console is turned away from the direction of the body,

between great wings of undulating contour that carry the curve of head and neck across the capital to the spiral volutes. The body forms a graceful reversed S, covered by fine imbrications in very low relief. The feathers of wings and body are rendered by different scale, tongue, curved-dart, and banded patterns. The right leg has been mutilated, but it is clear from the fragments that the powerful mass of the tail at the left was balanced by the two unequal legs. To this relief the impost ornament is especially adapted. The upper band of palmettes in low relief (the only palmette-

Fig. 65. Cloister; Capital of North Gallery: The Crusaders—Angel before Jerusalem

47

Fig. 66.
Cloister; Capital
at Corner of
East Gallery:
The Visitation

ornamented upper impost band in the cloister) is carved like the ornamental wings and other feathery surfaces of the eagle, while the lower group of symmetrically adossed lions with knotted tails above the eagle's head has a plastic energy and movement completely in accord with the symbolic bird. They parallel beautifully the outstretched wings.

Of all the sculptors of the cloister the master of the south gallery capitals was the boldest in his groupings and undertook the most difficult problems. He, more than any of the others, sought asymmetry even where the subject permitted a simpler arrangement, and delighted in elaborating the draperies of a figure to enrich its surface, its contours, and movement.[82] In the scene of Peter before Herod (Fig. 78) the latter is so majestically enthroned, the articulation of the figure

is so complex, that in the composition he takes up half the field; two standing figures are required to balance his great mass. The extended arms and legs form a strong scaffolding together with the flying folds at the ankle. The arc of the rich, beaded rosette medallion which serves as a throne repeats the arch behind his head—a fragment of architecture that signifies an interior—and is further echoed in the central festooning between the volute bands and Peter's nimbus. The figure is modeled and built in several layers, and behind the high relief of the body with its enveloping costume are the less salient flat surfaces of these accessories and of suspended draperies, the mantle with radiating folds under Herod's left arm.

The archaic features noted in this description cannot be said to arise from the need to reproduce complicated natural forms with an inadequate technique or limited knowledge of the forms. For the purely ornamental capitals show similar conceptions even in details not borrowed directly from nature. The foliate capitals of Corinthian type are subdivided into blocks of salient leaves; but on each of these blocks are cut separate leaves detached from each other, and without organic correspondence to the main salient mass. What in the classic prototype was a large curled leaf is in Moissac an assembly of several leaves each distinguished from its neighbor. In the classic capital the adjoining leaves overlapped so that the whole wrapping of foliage was luxuriant and free; but in Moissac the masses are isolated, their forms distinct, and the ornamental geometric structure more obvious. The single lobes of a leaf have the same relation to the leaf that the latter has to the salient mass, and this mass to the whole capital. The ornament is not free, sporadic, natural, but strictly organized with an apparent structure that dominates every turn and interval.[83] Nowhere in Moissac is the Roman Corinthian capital reproduced as faithfully as in Burgundy and Provence.

The decorative character of the figured compositions has been overlooked by French scholars who have conceded it in plant and animal capitals, where it is obvious. There the absence of iconographic significance, the traditional employment of such motifs as ornament, and the unmistakable simplicity and order of their schemes elicited instant recognition of the decorative conception. But the more complex design of the figures has not been understood because the arbitrariness of the groupings and the frequent distortion are opposed to the methods of later realistic art, and are judged to be products of inexperience and naiveté. Yet the rare figures mingled with some of the animals, and the few animal groups on the historiated capitals should have pointed to the fundamental unity of the narrative and decorative art. Monsieur Deschamps, who has studied the cloister *in situ*, nevertheless writes: "*c'est seulement aux frises stylisées, aux motifs purement décoratifs dont la composition se répète et demande moins d'invention, que nos sculpteurs ont su donner une réelle beauté. Mais quand il s'agit de composer, de grouper une scène autour de la corbeille d'un chapiteau, comme alors on voit leur inexpérience!*"[84]

In the constant coordination of gestures, movement, and contours with the volute bands of the capital and the triangle carved at their junction under the center console we see again how the abstract design is a primary consideration. For these are elements foreign to reality, survivals of the Corinthian capital which has been cleared of its foliage to make place for narrative figures; it is significant for the style of the capitals that this upper frame is a zigzag, symmetrical structure. In more realistic Romanesque and Gothic works, in which geometric design is less rigorously pursued, the figures are not coordinated with such accessories (and are often surmounted by an even more irregular frame). On the figured capitals of the porch of Moissac there are no volutes, consoles, or triangular central borders.

* * * * *

Having observed the abstract character of the design of these capitals, in which all figures and accessories are contrived in simple rhythmical forms, sometimes approaching the schematic patterning of pure ornament, we are not surprised that the backgrounds are neutral, and that the sacred stories are presented through actors in no particular space or environment, as in primitive pictographic writing. Locality is indicated only when it is an essential element of the legend, traditionally cited, or an accessory that gives meaning to figures otherwise undistinguished. The gate of Paradise is thus introduced the city of Bethlehem set between the Adoration of the Magi and the Massacre of the Innocents, and Jerusalem represented in the scene of the Crusaders (Fig. 65). But these cities are not a background against which the figures are placed. They do not cover the drum of the capital as their size would demand. They are separate items of

Fig. 67. Cloister; Capital of East Gallery: Lazarus and Dives

narrative as small as the figures or only a little larger, and are often only parts of a building or city—a tower, a house or wall—abbreviated to signify a greater whole.

Interiors are barely conceived by the artist. For an interior implies an enwalled hollow that effaces the background and introduces an extended third dimension. The sculptors of the cloister think in terms of separately aligned solid objects united by a common narrative context and an ornamental design rather than by their enclosure in a common deep space in nature. In banquet scenes like the Feast of Herod (Fig. 2) and the Marriage at Cana (Fig. 30), and in the group of Dives and Lazarus (Fig. 67), there is no definition of the limits of an action which must have taken place within a house. The only indication of an interior space is an arched frame or horizontal banding present behind figures in several capitals. It appears in the Feast of Herod, the Annunciation (Figs. 31, 66), and the Miracle of Cana (Fig. 52) but hardly evokes a distinct space or locality.[85]

The spacelessness of the narrative scenes is more radical than one would suppose from a first glance at the capitals. For the figures are often lively, well articulated, bulky, and abound in natural details; they seduce us into a belief in the reality of their whole setting and interrelation. But we observe soon that if they are set against no interior or exterior wall, even a supporting ground is absent, and finally that the conception of a definite horizontal plane is foreign to the early sculptors of Moissac.

The figures do not usually stand on a ground plane perpendicular to themselves. Most often the feet are carved upon the same vertical surface of the drum as the rest of the body, so that the figures appear suspended. Only rarely is the projecting astragal utilized as a ground plane; and when this is done, as in the Marriage of Cana, it is not on the upper horizontal side of the astragal that the feet are placed, but on its vertical surface, so that the feet are still presented as hanging.[86]

This lack of horizontal planes is also evident in the representation of chairs and tables. In the banquet scenes (Figs. 2, 30, 67) the upper surface of a table is parallel to the background and the figures, yet dishes and food are carved resting upon it. This projection of horizontal surfaces upon a vertical plane is consistently applied; even the seats and cushions are erected behind figures rather than beneath them (Virgin, in the Adoration of the Magi, Fig. 36; Daniel, Figs. 69, 86; Abraham and Lazarus, Fig. 68).[87]

Where the sculptor wishes to indicate that two figures are in depth one behind the other, he superposes them, or at least some of their limbs. In the Raising of Lazarus the method recalls old Oriental zoned perspective (Fig. 70). The two women who kneel before Christ are placed one above the other, and the upper seems to float in the air.[88] Likewise, in the Annunciation to the Shepherds (Fig. 32) three animals are superposed, without overlapping. In the capital of the Magi the foreparts of three horses emerge from the central tower which an inscription tells us is Jerusalem. The tower is so small that it could not possibly contain the concealed parts of the

Fig. 68. Cloister; Capital of East Gallery: Lazarus in Abraham's Bosom

Fig. 69. Cloister; Capital of North Gallery: Daniel

*Fig. 70.
Cloister; Capital
of West Gallery:
The Raising of
Lazarus*

*Fig. 71.
Cloister; Capital
of North Gal-
lery: Peter Heals
the Lame Man
at the Beautiful
Gate*

animals. They are set one above the other; the most distant is the highest, and his legs are suspended in the middle of the capital on no perceivable ground.

The figures, as jointed bodies capable of movement in three dimensions, are subject to related deforma‐ tions. The horizontal plane formed by the lap and thighs of a seated person is ignored and the legs are extended in profile (Abraham and Lazarus, Fig. 68; Daniel, Fig. 69; Apostles in the Washing of the Feet, etc.). In the frontal Virgin and Child of the Adora‐ tion (Fig. 36), this process is especially evident. The seat of the Virgin, as well as the cushion, is a vertical plane; the Child is applied parallel to the lower body of the Virgin, whose legs do not project to provide a seat for him, and his own legs, also without a lap, are in profile. Sometimes, as in the banquet scenes, a table conceals the supposedly extended legs of the seated figures (Figs. 2, 30). The rear leg of Herod, who is seated in profile, is carved above the front one instead of behind it, as in the superposed horses on the same capital (Fig. 35).

The gesturing hands are also drawn parallel to the surface of the capital rather than perpendicular or

*Fig. 72.
Cloister; Capital
of South Gal-
lery: Golias (the
Devil), Og, and
Magog*

diagonal to it. The limbs are pressed close to the wall
or the body; and in this uniform striving for clarity in
the itemized legible representation of separate parts,
the profiles of extended limbs are preferred to less
distinct views. If the feet in some capitals hang vertically, in others a standing figure has both feet in
strict profile and parted at a straight angle to each
other (Virgin of Annunciation, Fig. 31). The vertical
frontal feet permit a view of their full unforeshortened form. But this is possible even in profile. Adam
before the reproachful Lord stands with feet in profile
and with their entire upper surface clearly visible, as
if the soles were planted on the wall itself (Fig. 40).
The hands, too, as in the pier reliefs, are limited to
those gestures which least obscure their complete
form. They are most often carved flat against the

background, with little or no foreshortening.

It would be wrong to suppose that all conception of
depth is lacking. There is no enclosed space, no sharp
contrast of ground, foreground, and background, and
there are no movements in depth as free as those on
the vertical pictorial surface. But by differences of
relief, by the modeling of bodies and the occasional
overlapping of parts, limited effects of three-dimensional space are produced.

By the salience of the figures from the background
and the uniform projection of the astragal as a ledge
around the surface, a narrow stage is created for the
action. The overhanging console and impost suggest
the same depth above. The relatively high relief of
the figures—for they are very small and quite salient—admits a contrast of light and dark and a layer-

ing of several surfaces on the capital. The figure is enveloped by shells of drapery which constitute distinct surfaces; in places they are extended across the background in a series of planes between the figure and the wall. On capitals of the south gallery such drapes are enriched by pleats and undercutting, and the interval between the foreground and background is bridged by numerous surfaces. The latter are usually parallel to each other, but in some cases, as in the seated figure of Daniel in the north gallery (Fig. 69), they are contrasted in section—concave opposed to convex—with the suggestion of a more considerable depth. A few figures are even partly detached from the background, as if there were a space behind them, but these are exceptional (Fig. 93). They remain significant, however, as a variation anticipating later art.

Another source of spatial suggestion is the overlapping of figures and objects. Such encroachment of parts may be seen in the capital of the Miracle of St. Benedict (Fig. 41); figures stand behind rather than beside the recumbent person. In the Liberation of Peter (Fig. 81) and in other capitals of the south gallery such overlapping is especially pronounced, and is not merely an unavoidable consequence of the theme or the restricted surface, but seems to be a predilection of an artist with a more complex style than the others. In the Miracle of Peter, on a capital of the north gallery (Fig. 71), by a sculptor of especially refined style, the Beautiful Gate of Jerusalem is represented behind the figure of the lame man as an actual background. This implies a spatial conception of relief more advanced than in the other capitals. But this innovation is treated in an archaic manner, for the building is parallel to the figure and the surface of the capital, and the relation of figure and architecture is not confirmed by a ground plane common to the two. Here again we find an anticipation of later art, associated with precocious lettering and a more complex asymmetrical composition than appears on the other capitals of the cloister.

There occur also occasional movements perpendicular or diagonal to the background, notably in the south gallery. The arms of Christ in the Temptation (Fig. 84), of the symbol of Matthew (Fig. 63), and of the figure of Asaph in the capital of David's Musicians are more boldly foreshortened. On a capital engaged to the northeast pier—of St. Michael fighting the dragon—a central orant figure stands with left leg flexed in a manner unusual in the cloister (Fig. 73). It reminds us of the relaxed legs of classical statues. The effectiveness of such movements is limited since they

are so rare and isolated; no accessories prolong them or help to fix the spatial relation more precisely.

Sometimes a figure is so related to architecture that we infer unseen spaces. On the capital of the Magi (Fig. 35) the three horses emerge from a tower. An innkeeper stands in a doorway in the parable of the Good Samaritan (Fig. 59). The apocalyptic monster, Golias (Fig. 72), issues from a building so high in relief that the doorway is carved in the thickness of the building, i.e., on a plane perpendicular to the background.

But a linear perspective is unknown. There is no attempt to represent a depth more extensive than the actual thickness of the relief; and if the narrow lair of the monster Golias is rendered in depth, it is by means of an approximation to sculpture in the round rather than by foreshortening or atmospheric devices. The treatment of architecture, which is so abundantly represented on the capitals of this cloister that a treatise on Romanesque construction might be illustrated by them, shows this clearly. When whole buildings are introduced they are placed beside the figures rather than behind them. Houses and figures are of about the same height, and are usually set on the same plane in equal salience (Figs. 41, 53, 65, etc.).

Only one broad face of a building is shown in its entirety and is parallel to the background plane. Plunging or angular viewpoints are avoided; but by an adjustment which is characteristic of this art, with its concept of completeness, the roof is as visible to us as the lower doorway. The buildings—religious, domestic, and civil—are minutely observed and detailed. The profiles of arch moldings, the jointed masonry, and even the small parts of door bolts are rendered.

*Fig. 73.
Cloister; Capital at Corner of North Gallery: St. Michael and the Dragon*

But the more evident plan is usually distorted because of the lack of foreshortening and broad planes perpendicular to each other. Such neighboring surfaces are set at an angle approaching 180 degrees, as in the drawings of children, primitives, and self-taught moderns who indicate the adjoining sides of a building as if on one plane.[89] And as in such drawings, we observe in the representations of Jerusalem (Fig. 65) and of Cana (Fig. 30) three sides of a rectangular structure at the same time. It is this deformation that gives these buildings the appearance of a polygonal plan. The sculptor wished to present as many sides as possible, but to retain the angularity proper to them.

The upper stories or towers are often set back as if in real space, but hardly in effective proportion to the actual recession of such members. In the treatment of such details and of the sides of these buildings we can grasp the conceptual character of the space world of these capitals. The buildings are essentially facades, elevations rendered in exceedingly low relief. The sides are narrow walls which disappear into the background of the capital without foreshortening or indication of the actual depth of the structure. The building appears to be a wall applied to the surface or emerging from the impenetrable interior of the capital.

The high relief convinces us of the bulk and projection of figures, but not of their full detachment from the background surface of the capital or their penetration into it. Relief and background are not entirely distinct. The latter cannot be considered a

wall before which the figures move as on a stage (although this is already intimated on a few capitals of the south gallery); the movements are strictly parallel to the background, as if they were bound to it in some way. The apparent indefiniteness of the space arises from the lack of horizontal planes and a distinct ground. We cannot identify it with either the restricted but definite platform of Gothic reliefs and paintings, or the boundless but undifferentiated space of expressive, religious import evoked in Early Christian and Byzantine art. Since the background is simply the surface of the object on which the figures are represented and is not itself a representation, it has no symbolic value, like the uniform gold or blue background of figures in a mosaic. It is genuinely neutral, as in the early Greek reliefs which combine a similar architectonic-decorative parallelism of surfaces with a design of analogous simplicity and a related manner of conceiving natural forms part by part in their most general aspect.

The material character of this background is evidenced in its broken upper surface of volutes, consoles, and central triangles. These are parts of the object decorated (the capital), rather than represented spatial elements. The fact that they enter decisively into the design does not change this character, since the design is decorative and includes the surfaces and shapes of the decorated object.

But this succession of layered surfaces between the impost and astragal itself constitutes a spatial system. The console emerges from a greater depth than the volutes and is often carved in several planes, including surfaces at an angle to the capital. The volute bands are molded in two planes, while the triangle between them is sometimes modeled. Hence the head of Nebuchadnezzar (Fig. 74) under the console seems to advance from a remoter space. It is placed in front of three overlapping surfaces, one of which—the console—is subdivided into two angular planes and projects from a deeper wall. The figure, because of the relief and the considerable succession of parts—the arms, sleeves, body, cushion, and seat—seems to sit before a wall rather than emerge from it. The diagonal surface of the console also suggests a freer shaping of the space of the whole.[90] The spatial element here is not simply a representation but a decorative contrivance, and is significant for the later elaboration of the sculptured frame as a space-building factor. But the indenting and projections of the upper part of the capital by volutes and consoles are essentially foreign to the narrative aim, which seems to call for a clear

Fig. 74. Cloister; Capital of South Gallery: Nebuchadnezzar

and consistent delimitation of the field of the figures, whereas on these capitals that field is irregular and layered and in several places the figures cross the volutes or the consoles. Such frames are not inconsistent, however, with a lively expression of action for which the representation is coordinated in its lines and masses with frequently trespassed irregular boundaries, independent of nature or the subject.

Thus the effect of these modeled, massive figures and accessories remains that of an arbitrary assemblage of separate signs which to a great degree accord in appearance with their specific reference. But a more extended activity in depth through bodily movement is denied them. They are like shadows cast on a wall, or the repeated units of an ornamental frieze. Although they represent incidents of which the actors and accessories are drawn from a real world, it is another logic of space and movement that governs them.

These characteristics of the space and perspective of the Moissac cloister are interesting not only in themselves and because of their intimate connection with certain aesthetic results, but also because some of them appear in other civilizations and times remote from eleventh-century Languedoc, and precede the development of three-dimensional representation in more recent art. The approach to an imaginary space in art as extended as that of our actual world was a slow process, without the sudden propulsion that might result from the intrusion, in pictorial imagination, of our everyday habitual awareness of how distant objects differ from near and how a varying sunlight affects the appearance of familiar forms. The artistic conception involves a positive process which represents objects to suit an existing style and an immediate decorative end. It is from the elements already represented that a constructed space will begin to emerge in the next generation of Languedoc sculptors. There will be no radical revision of the style to accommodate a newly apprehended concept; but the overlapping, modeling, and embryonic perspective will yield a slightly more plausible penetra-

Fig. 75.
Cloister; Capital of East Gallery: The Washing of Feet

tion of depth, as proportions become less arbitrary, and the movement and modeling of figures call for a clearer definition of ground, foreground, and background.

It is significant that in this group of capitals, executed in a short period, the spatial features described are not uniform; they show small variations which point to later art, just as do the details of representation in the cloister piers. This fact throws light not only on the history of forms but on their character as well, for we learn from it that the forms or processes were not absolutely stable. The diversity may indicate the cooperation of artists of different ages, but there is presupposed, in that case, a developing style. Even on the same capital, however, we can observe the primitive vertical projection of members and a more advanced procedure. The innovations do not imply a consistent revision of the whole style.

THE FIGURES OF THE CLOISTER CAPITALS

In an earlier chapter were described the figures of apostles placed singly on large flat surfaces. We turned then to smaller sculptures of which the groupings of figures were considered. Now we may ask: Are the individual figures of the capitals similar to those of the piers? How are they affected by the smaller scale, a different material, and another technique of cutting? How are they influenced by the narrative content of the capitals? Does the greater variety of forms in the more numerous capitals indicate a development in time or the presence of several sculptors of differing skill or tradition?

On some capitals there are figures which in posture

Fig. 76. Cloister; Capital at Corner of South Gallery: Baptism of Christ

and in the design of their garments are almost precise replicas of the apostles on the adjacent piers. Such is the angel at the left of the Sacrifice of Isaac (Fig. 55). St. Michael in the north gallery and a figure of St. John on the nearby capital, representing a miracle of Peter, also recall the apostles (Fig. 71). The diagonal line of the mantle, extending from the ankle to the waist, is as common on the capitals as on the piers. As on the latter, concentric folds, incised and doubled, issue from this diagonal line. On the capital may also be seen the contrast of the uncovered side of the tunic, with its vertical leg folds, and the broad striated surface of the mantle. The peculiar curved incision at the exposed knee, the little patterned break of the lower horizontal edge, the slinglike enclosure of the arm in imitation of classic art, and the parallel torso folds, all these occur on the capitals.[91]

But because of the smaller size of the figures an equal delicacy was not so readily achieved. The interval between two grooves of a fold seems clumsy on the capitals, refined on the larger piers. The common details, especially of folds and features, stand out much more prominently in the smaller works. This is not due to a difference of skill, but to the nature of the tools and surfaces. In Chartres, also, the transfer of the forms of the jamb figures on the west portal to the capitals above them entailed a similar change.

The same depth of relief cutting on the piers and on the capitals is clearly of different significance because of the size of the figures. The salience of two or three inches of a figure only eight to twelve inches high is massive and suggests an almost total emergence from the wall; but on one of the apostles, almost five feet tall, the effect is of scant relief, if not of drawing. The difference is especially evident in the treatment of the head. Even when turned in profile, the head on the capital is rendered in its full mass, like sculpture in the round; when seen from the side, it presents a full face to the spectator. But for the actual modeling of the head, the relatively higher relief is of less consequence. These smaller figures do not manifest a more developed study of the head structure than do the figures on the piers.[92] On the contrary, as we should expect, the delicacy of facial surface and the fine detail of the features, possible on the larger heads of the apostles, are reduced on most of the capitals.

It is only on some capitals of the south gallery that the smaller scale does not result in a relatively thickened reproduction of the forms of the apostles. The folds are as delicate as on the latter, and insofar as a

Fig. 77.
Cloister; Capital
of East Gallery:
The Souls of the
Three Spanish
Saints in Glory

greater variety of forms appears in them, it may be said that on these capitals the work is even more refined than on the piers. The chiseling of the ordinary stone produces here transitions and undercutting not attempted on the larger marble slabs of the piers. The coincidence of this novel technique with a more complex design and space and with forms anticipating later Romanesque styles indicates that materials or tools alone cannot account for the difference from the other works of the cloister; an artist, influenced by other traditions, more "modern" in his time, and more ambitious, was at work here.

On the other hand, in some capitals, like the Washing of Feet (Fig. 75), the forms of the pier reliefs are immobilized, simplified and thickened even more than on the capitals first discussed. The capital itself is more massive, broader at the base, than the others. The eyes of the figures bulge enormously; their hands and feet are immense; the few lines of drapery seem to swathe the figures which are exceedingly squat. The apostles on this capital are only three heads in height. If the capitals of the south gallery seem the work of an artist other than the master of the pier reliefs because of more highly differentiated forms, this capital seems the work of still another by virtue of its distinct simplicity and more pronounced archaism.

That squatness appears surprising to us until we recall other primitive arts which present an equally unhuman canon. Even classic art, which at one time placed so great a value upon height as a mark of strength and dignity, in its last phases reduced the figures to stunted pygmies, far from human, much more from heroic, proportions. Such are the men carved in the early fourth century on the Arch of Constantine to celebrate the victories of an emperor; such also are the saints and Biblical figures on some Christian sarcophagi.

The shepherds in the west gallery (Fig. 32), the figures on the accompanying capitals that represent the Raising of Lazarus and the Anointing of David (Fig. 85) are not much taller. Even on the capitals carved with greater skill the head remains unusually large. In the desire to indicate all that is essential to the structure of the head which already figures so largely in the conception of a man, the sculptor has given it a disproportionate physical prominence. The torso and legs, covered by draperies, are defined by fewer details. If we regard only the parts of the body below the shoulders of the nude Spanish martyrs (Fig. 77), their proportions will appear normal, though marked by forms which have been arbitrarily simplified. But if we include the heads, then the figures will appear stunted and deformed.

In the capitals the heads of children and adults are of one size. This is not a gross error of representation, when the proportions of the whole body are considered. In the Massacre of the Innocents (Fig. 37) the adults are only three or four heads in height, and the children, two. Also the heads of women and men are not distinguished in mass, except where a beard gives the male head a greater surface. Their bodies too are of one size. We cannot regard these proportions as absolutes since the isocephalism of primitive relief plays an important role in determining size. The heads of seated and standing figures are usually on the same level. The seated figures therefore seem more naturalistically proportioned (Fig. 78). Sometimes, perhaps in avoidance of the odd proportions of legs and head inevitable in a seated figure whose head is on the same level as that of a standing figure, the feet are made to hang like a baby's. But actually, where the narrative calls for subordination, the figures are not of equal height. So the baptized Christ (Fig. 76) is sunk into the water up to his breast; his head is below John's. The same observation may be made of Isaac in the sacrifice (Fig. 55), of Abel attacked by Cain, and of a servant at Herod's feast (Fig. 2).

These peculiarities of proportion occur also in the capitals of the south gallery, which are in other respects more refined in detail and more natural than

Fig. 78.
Cloister; Capital of South Gallery: Peter before Herod

the adjoining capitals. The standing figure never attains a height of more than five heads.

Like the apostles of the piers, the figures on the capitals are disposed by the artist to yield as clear views as possible of their important parts—head, hands, and feet—despite the consequent distortion. The figures of Adam and the Lord (Fig. 40) are good examples of this archaic conception and are especially worth a closer observation because of their contrasted dress and nudity. Both heads have been destroyed. Enough of the necks and the contours of the heads is preserved to assure us that the heads were in profile, facing each other as the narrative demanded. Yet the shoulders of both are strictly frontal as in Egyptian drawing and relief; likewise the torsos, except that in Adam the nudity permits us to see the abdomen, of which the sculptor has wished to suggest the roundness by a curved contour. This distortion of the abdomen of a frontal torso, in order to represent its profile, appears in many other figures of the cloister, even in the clothed. If we do not observe it on the Lord it is because the abdomen is covered by his hand.

But once the groin is reached the artist abandons the frontality of his figure, for his legs are best seen in profile. The nakedness here betrays a process less evident in the clothed figures. Adam's hand and leaf conceal a junction difficult to realize in a figure so arbitrarily twisted. If his legs are in profile, how can we see both of them unless one is advanced? And, as in Assyrian art, it is the remote leg that is brought forward. To render the right foot behind the left, they are superposed; but the big toe of the left foot, the lower one, overlaps a toe of the right—a naive version of the concealment of one by the other in our vision of a profile figure in nature. Both feet are laid out on the surface of the capital as if seen from above or planted on a wall.

The Lord's left (rear) leg is also bent so that it may be seen in profile. Both feet are suspended in parallel rather than divergent diagonals and are exposed in their full unforeshortened mass.

If we examine now the proportioning of the various parts we shall conclude that here too is at work a process of abstraction, fractioning, and addition such as has arbitrarily twisted the axes of the body. The hands of Adam are enormous. The open, extended left hand lies across the whole length of the thigh. The closed right fist is longer than the breast. The proportions of head and body have been noted before. Here they are exposed in the naked figure in which

the drapery, essentially subordinate to our conception of man's body and in itself undifferentiated in scale by fixed units (as of limbs, torso, etc.), does not conceal from us the sculptor's conception of the whole figure. In simple recollection of the nude body the shoulders are distinct from the breast. The sculptor has therefore given shoulders and breast equal prominence, with great exaggeration of the former, but has not indicated the clavicle. But from breast to foot the body is proportioned as in the most common type of West European man. Were it not for the hands, the shoulders, and the head, we would feel no excessive disproportion.

The sculptor's conception is not of a characteristic body contour, but of the combined shapes of separate limbs and large masses, like the abdomen. These he represents in a simple form which admits no specific muscles or bony structure and no subtle indentations of surface and outline. Although the hands and head are grossly enlarged, the body axis distorted, and the stance of the figure so improbable, care is taken to represent the navel and nipples, which appear as decorative surface elements. The obvious pattern of the ribs could hardly have escaped an artist so devoted to

Fig. 79. Cloister; Capital of South Gallery: David's Musicians, Ethan and Idithun

decorative abstraction. They have a skeletal prominence in a body of which the other bones are not even suggested. Following the costal margin as a guide, the sculptor arbitrarily arranged them in a chevron pattern, with the sternum at the apex, in reversal of the true direction. The ascending curve of the ribs toward the back is not observed, perhaps because of the more complex form; such an observation implies foreshortening and attention to planes perpendicular to the main body surface, both foreign to this sculptor.

The broad surfaces of the chest and abdomen are flat or curved slightly, without abrupt transitions. Arms and legs are simple rounded members with no apparent articulation at the joints. The meeting of limbs is a simple angle of the contour, a slight break or incision of the surface, precisely as in the jointless hands. In the left leg of Adam the rear profile is suavely curved in recognition of an obvious musculature which is not otherwise indicated. The surface of a male body is therefore hardly different from that of a female; we must see them clothed in order to distinguish them. The distinction is, in fact, difficult in the scene of the Temptation (Fig. 34). Only the longer hair of the right figure permits us to call it Eve. We see more clearly here the confusion of front and profile of the abdomen, the prominence of the head and hands, the lack of muscular differentiation, the contrast of profile legs and head with the frontal shoulders. The sexless nude souls of Peter and Paul (Fig. 45) in the same gallery are remarkably like Adam and Eve.

Not all nude figures are treated in this manner. The exceptional symmetry and frontal position of Durand, which were explained by his episcopal and monastic rank and by the commemorative nature of the relief, occur in many nude figures on the capitals. Sometimes they are motivated by religious meanings, as in the nude soul of the martyred Saturninus who stands alone in the mandorla on a background of two convergent sets of radial lines (Fig. 46). Were it not for the extremities, the body would have the normal human proportions. It is precisely designed, in perfect symmetry; the hands are extended alike, and both sides of the figure are identical in their delicately curved contours. The ribs are patterned, unlike Adam's, in well-observed concentric lines.

On the neighboring capital of the Spanish martyrs, the mandorla is filled by the three nude orant souls (Fig. 77). The limited surface has required the squeezing of the lateral figures into narrow corners, the slight turn of their bodies, and the overlapping of the inner sides of those two martyrs by the central soul. In the soft unmodeled bodies with rounded limbs the ribs are coarsely incised, and even the clavicle is rendered by a thick ridge at the base of the neck, converging to the sternum.

Another symmetrical standing nude appears on an ornamental carving in the west gallery, grasping the wings of two dragons. The motif is repeated on all four faces of the capital. Although by the same hand, the figures are not identically proportioned and modeled. The ribs, ridged in one, are faintly incised in another. But all have a common pose and a similar beauty of line and surface.

Besides these figures there are nude demons (Fig. 42), the half-dressed beggar in the capital of St. Martin (Fig. 54), and a partly nude personification of a Beatitude in the west gallery. The profile position of the devil who receives the offering of Cain is unusual in the cloister (Fig. 93).[93] It governs the whole figure and not merely the legs and head. The shoulders are perpendicular to the surface of the capital. The contour of the back of the neck and the head has been carefully noted, while the ribs, in relief, are not the symmetrical structures of the other capitals, but the well-observed forms of the side of the body. Unfortunately, the lower limbs of this demon, who approaches human shape more closely than the human figures of the cloister, are badly mutilated; we cannot tell how the sculptor made the transition from human to animal form plausible. Unlike the figure of Adam, the demon has the outer leg advanced, almost com-

Fig. 80.
Cloister; Detail
of Decorative
Capital

pletely detached from the background. This double departure from archaic methods perhaps explains its destruction. The undercut and detached outer arms of both Cain and the demon have also been destroyed.

The unusual forms observed in this capital are not isolated details of the style, but elements of an increasing refinement apparent in the technique, proportions, folds, and movements, and even the inscriptions. The wheat offered by Cain is placed on the altar under the console, each blade finely rendered and the whole forming a column and capital, reminiscent of the ancient Egyptian. In the persistent symmetry of the group, the squatness of the figures, the large heads (but tiny feet), and the common drapery conventions, we see that the exceptional details of this sculpture are not intrusions of another style but developments from the more archaic forms of the cloister. The demon who tempts Christ in the south gallery (Fig. 84), on a capital which shows forms of drapery genuinely new in the cloister, is more archaic than the demon before Cain. Here, too, the frontality of the upper body persists.

Besides these standing nude figures there are others in less common positions. In the parable of Dives, Lazarus is stretched out horizontally across two sides of the capital, forming an arc of ninety degrees in plan (Fig. 67). He furnishes a remarkable instance of the arbitrary space of the world of these capitals. Though obviously recumbent, he is carved lying on the vertical surface rather than on the astragal only a trifle below him. His body is presented frontally, as if seen directly from above, the whole torso unforeshortened. The upper body is long and slender, the legs almost nonexistent in their shortness. As in the representation of tables in the cloister capitals, the hori-

zontal surface of the recumbent figure has been projected vertically.

* * * * *

In the study of the piers we observed that the heads of the apostles were individual conceptions, like portraits, although so uniform in their surfaces. In the case of Durand, a Cluniac tradition (that speaks of his jesting nature) has been cited to confirm the accuracy of the equivocal expression in his likeness. Yet this is surely the stiffest of the figures, the most schematically constructed and ornamental.

The smaller scale of the capitals hardly admitted such fine distinction of personalities. The head of St. John the Evangelist in the south gallery (Fig. 56) is an exception, and less surprising when the more elaborate detail of other figures in this gallery is considered.

The impassivity of the apostles is an expression proper to their hieratic positions and gestures. But the absence of facial expression in scenes of violence like the Martyrdoms, the Massacre of the Innocents, and the Entry of the Crusaders into Jerusalem is especially remarkable. When we recall the contemporary anonymous historian's account of this last event (Fig. 49), in which religious fervor followed an unrestrained brutality that made Tancred weep, and when we remember also the enthusiasm of the convocations, the impassivity of the scene is astonishing. Such "serenity" is not limited to the early art of

Fig. 81. Cloister; Capital of South Gallery: Liberation of Peter

Fig. 82. Cloister; Capital of West Gallery: The Beatitudes

Greece, but is a common archaic feature. The expression of the faces on the capitals is neutral rather than impassive. There is a total absence of facial expression beyond the smile of the little demon (?) behind Herod in the Massacre of the Innocents (Fig. 35). The representation of a momentary feeling is foreign to this art which proceeds from the more stable or general appearance of individual objects.

Expressiveness is achieved by other means. Either symbolical gestures, movements, and attributes communicate their feelings and characters, or the design of the work, the zigzag or calmer organization of forms, sometimes expresses the quality of an episode or situation. The latter is most evident in the hieratic groups of saints and angels, in which symmetry and centralized design confer the effect of a ritual moment and a dogmatic finality on the representation. This result is of course not separable from specific attributes like haloes and mandorlas and from gestures that symbolize exaltation or prayer.

On the capital of the Martyrdom of the Three Spanish Saints, Fructuosus, Augurius, and Eulogius, the composition of each of the four scenes has a distinct expressive character. First they stand in their ecclesiastic robes in ceremonious postures, strictly frontal (Fig. 33); then they appear in the flames, nude and orant, in a beautiful symmetrical design of wavy flames, maintained in their own gestures (Fig. 83). Despite the horrible theme there is no sense of violent engagement of the figures and the fire, but a common upward movement, as of flowers emerging from a thick base of stems and long curved foliage. The adjoining scene of the prefect Emilianus commanding the execution has a more genuinely broken, exciting form, with many angles and strong oppositions throughout the field (Fig. 97). The official sits on an X-shaped chair, before a musician with a triangular instrument. The former's garment is divided by folds into several triangles. His arm extends diagonally across the middle of the surface, and ends in a pointing finger. Three leaves curled over the tip of the central triangle of the frame produce a more insistent zigzag above. The contour of the musician provides another zigzag line, which is paralleled in the forms of two men at the left who stir the flames with diagonal rods. To increase this effect of sustained diagonal contrasts the sculptor has broken the volute bands by numerous short diagonal lines, saw-toothed in section. Even the astragal has a prominent pattern of intersecting diagonal strands. On the fourth side of the capital (Fig. 77), the souls of the three nude martyrs are enclosed in the middle of the field by a jeweled mandorla held above by the hand of God and at the sides by two angels. By the greater mass of the central figure, by lines concentric with the mandorla incised behind the saints, by the related forms of the angels and their wings, and by the four hands of the saints placed palm outward across the middle of the field, the composition acquires a more definite centrality and seems to focus on the glory of the martyrs.

Such coordination of expressive form and content is not everywhere apparent. It throws some light on Romanesque methods of design and independence of purely material factors, like the shape of a field, and the traditional iconographic data. On no two sides of this capital of the Spanish martyrs do we find identical frames. The upper zigzag is modified to accord with a conception of the whole surface; sometimes the volute bands are striated, sometimes the central triangle is omitted or topped by foliage.

The individual gestures are very few in number and thoroughly conventional. Most frequently, the hand is extended, either pointing or palm outward, as a symbol of acknowledgment, prayer, surprise, or speech. The orant arms of the three Hebrews and the three Spanish martyrs are a deliberately applied symbol of the cross as well as a gesture (and in the Romanesque period, artistic symbol) of prayer. In the figure of Durand, the hand is raised stiffly in an emphatic gesture of commanding speech which has become the static sign of his spiritual authority. In some figures the legs are crossed, but the meaning of this posture is not clear (Figs. 64, 76, 97). It is the stance of a possessed figure in a miniature of the late eleventh century from Monte Cassino, but is more frequently found at this time in sacred figures. In Romanesque art it is an expressive formal device, an unstable, untectonic posture with parallels even in architecture, a strained movement and inward tension. In the cloister, it is still a convention without intensity.

On the more archaic capitals of the cloister each figure is engaged with a single object and refers to only one other figure in his gesture or movement. But on the capitals of the south gallery (and the north) the use of gesture is more complex. The sculptors were too archaic to link the action of figures by the glance of the eye; but through the positions of hands and heads they achieved a similar connection. I have already observed that in the Healing of the Centurion's Servant (Fig. 62), the centurion (facing Christ, who stands at the right) extends one hand to the left, pointing to the servant in bed, and addresses Christ by raising the right hand before him. Christ is turned to the right, away from the supplicating figure, but his head is directed to the centurion. There is created by these contrasting motions (the bent legs of Christ are an additional element of contrast) a complicated intercourse, in which the double preoccupation of each figure—the centurion's with his servant and with Christ, Christ's with the centurion and the apostles—is adequately expressed.[94]

On the capital of Nebuchadnezzar (Fig. 47) the figure who stands at the right is turned away from the king, though facing him; his opposed arms point in opposite directions. An analogous complexity may be observed in the king himself, whose arms are contrasted in gesture, the head turned, and even the legs crossed. The double gesture is not merely designed to represent a more complex interaction, but is an element of a style which promotes contrasts and movement. It constitutes an expressive form as well as an expressive symbol.

DRAPERY

The drapery forms of the capitals include all that were observed on the sculptures of the piers. The schematic incised radial, concentric, and elliptical folds, the doubled lines, the patterned breaks of the horizontal edges, all appear on the smaller figures. The difference in scale modifies the proportion of the fold to the whole figure, so that on an analogous apostle on a capital the drapery lines are fewer and the folds are considerably thickened. One detail of

Romanesque costume unknown on the piers is a commonplace on the figures of the capitals who wear contemporary dress. This is the vertical slit on the collar of the tunic at the sternum. On the capitals of the south gallery the jeweled ornament, carved on the borders of the garment of Durand and James, becomes an element of style and is applied on angels, kings, and lay figures of lesser rank. The peculiar definition of the folds of the lower abdomen by an ovoid figure with an incised horizontal axis, which occurs on several of the apostles on the piers, is often repeated on the smaller figures of the capitals. But on the latter this form is part of a larger system of folds which includes concentric bands drawn across the torso. These bands are less visible on the piers, perhaps because of the mantles which conceal the torso folds of the apostles, or because of the traditional ancient costume worn by the latter.

It is significant of the latent realism of this style that the costume of the figures on the capitals is minutely differentiated and offers a great variety of types. For not only apostles, but all kinds of secular figures—kings, soldiers, executioners, shepherds, musicians, servants, women, and children—and many religious types—saints, angels, martyrs, bishops,

Fig. 83. Cloister; Capital of East Gallery: The Three Spanish Saints in Flames

Fig. 84. Cloister; Capital of South Gallery: Temptation of Christ

prophets, monks, and priests—appear on these sculptures in distinct dress.

In one large group of capitals, including those of the north and west galleries—with the exception of those engaged to the piers and the capital representing the Annunciation to the Shepherds (Fig. 32)—and three western capitals of the south gallery (Nebuchadnezzar, Stephen, and Babylon, Figs. 47, 48, 74, 92), the forms of drapery are precisely those of the pier reliefs, without the addition of elements unknown in the latter. The differences are mainly of scale and costume. Even the figures in movement are governed by the same isolation of folds, clear contours, incised lines, and the close fitting of the garment to the actual contours of the body. The unmodeled clothes cover the figure like a shell. Except for the familiar pentagonal pattern on the lower edge, the outlines are usually simple and unbroken. It is only by exception that a slightly greater prominence

is given in a few instances to hanging or flaring parts of the costume.

On the capitals of the east gallery and those engaged to the piers, the forms described above persist, but are accompanied by others with different principles of drapery composition. Thus the plain diagonal of the mantle is broken by zigzag pleats, and the contour of the garment, ordinarily fitted to the body, is sometimes expanded by flying ends of drapery. On Nero's legs in the martyrdom of Peter and Paul (Fig. 87) the falling mantle cascades in pleats unknown on the piers. In addition to the common concentric incised lines a chevron system is employed to organize the folds on the body surface. The horizontal edge of the tunic of the angel who expels Adam and Eve (Fig. 39) is broken by a continuous wave pattern. But these new elements of drapery design are less refined in execution than the more usual forms of the north gallery. More often they are coarser and thicker, heav-

Fig. 85.
Cloister; Capital
of West Gallery:
The Anointing of
David

Fig. 86.
Cloister; Capital
of West Gallery:
Daniel in the
Lions' Den

Fig. 87.
Cloister; Capital
of East Gallery:
Martyrdom of
Peter and Paul—
Nero

ily ridged or grooved, and associated with figures of squat proportions.

A more striking and pervasive departure from the drapery types of the piers occurs in the ten historiated capitals of the eastern part of the south gallery. They differ from the other capitals in the greater richness of dress, in the complexity of folds, in the breaking of contours by the zigzag and meandering edges of pleats, in the multiplied overlapping folds, in the free use of flying and blown ends, in the more plastic surfaces of cloth, in the undercutting of the lower edge of the garment, and in the more refined treatment of those features of the other style which persist in the new. In these capitals we see conventions of drapery pattern common in the developed Romanesque style of the twelfth century.

The garment is less closely fitted to the body. It is not limited to the simple rectangular mass, adorned with radial and concentric lines, but is arbitrarily broken at the edges into lively patterns. A line recalling the Vitruvian scroll or "running dog" terminates the pleats on some figures. It approaches the meander in the reduction of the curves to straight or only slightly curved lines forming alternately obtuse and acute angles. It is a highly developed, late archaic form of which the relation to the far simpler folds of the east gallery will be more clearly grasped if we observe the parallel contrast in early Greek art of the vases of Euphronius and a late black-figured work. The few pleatings of the east gallery form simple zigzag contours, without the complexity of a meander or a scroll. Their surfaces are perfectly flat, just as their terminations are simple curves or unvaried straight lines. The pleating itself is broadly spaced and limited to three or four planes at the most.

The sculptor of the south gallery does not simply abstract from the normal pleating of unarranged folds an effect of parallel or radial banding and a lively scroll contour. The mantle or tunic is blown in different directions to generate such forms outside the boundaries of the body. The mantle of Herod (Fig. 78), hanging from his arm, is extended diagonally across the background and ornamented by a fine pattern of double incised radial lines, a few modeled pleats, and a wavy scroll contour. This extension of the mantle is not designed for such effects alone; it serves also to unite two parts of a composition otherwise unbalanced, and opposes a similar jutting of the mantle of Peter beside it. It suggests a comparison with the similarly extended mantles of the Magi (Fig. 36). The latter are plain and unbroken by multiplied folds.

The sculptor has yet other devices for accenting the movements of figures by the lines of their garments. At the left leg of Herod the tunic is blown far behind to form a curious horizontal process, consisting of a thin upper band, an outer polygonal fold

hooded to resemble a dome, a series of small vertical pleats of wavy lower contour, and several concentric sets of incised folds that connect this group with the main body of the garment. The same structure appears on the apocalyptic horseman (Fig. 61), where it is more obviously motivated by the movement of the figure, as in equestrian representations in Greek and Byzantine art. Sometimes a slender end of drapery flies from the back of the figure; sometimes the parallel pleatings on the body are carved in diagonals contrary to the direction of the other folds, as if blown from behind (Og and Magog—Fig. 72).

Another source of complex linear movement and plastic variation is the swathing of the figure in great garments, far exceeding the actual body surface. The dress on most of the capitals is more closely fitted than in the south gallery where the amplitude of costume allows the richest overlapping. On the apocalyptic angel with the sickle (Fig. 90) the outer garment is so large that it must be tucked under the lower tunic at the waist.

The polygonal pattern of the lower horizontal edge persists in these capitals, but is further developed in outline and modeling. It tends toward a more broken, yet more distinct contour, and is more plastically rendered. It terminates a fold no longer rigidly vertical, but irregular, curved, blown, and even triangular. In addition it is so employed in groups of three that the horizontal border becomes even more restless. In the Christ of the Transfiguration (Fig. 88) two such folds are directly superposed, like two vertical symmetrical zigzags united at the top by a horizontal line. This is a more complex form which appears frequently in later

Fig. 88. Cloister; Capital of South Gallery: Transfiguration of Christ

Fig. 89. Cloister; Capital of South Gallery: Christ and the Canaanite Woman—Apostles

Romanesque art.

Even the banded folds of the torso are elaborated. They are not simply doubled by parallel incision, but in some cases (Healing of the Centurion's Servant and the Canaanite Girl—Figs. 62, 89) each fold of the torso is accompanied by two such incisions.

It would be a mistake to suppose that in these capitals the draperies alone were enriched without a development of other features. Though very primitive forms persist here, their sculptor undertakes more complex compositions than any of his fellows. His surfaces are carved with greater variety. He employs jeweled ornament in a profusion that suggests the later and more monumental tympanum. His buildings are distinguished among all those represented in the cloister by their refined detail and by exotic types like the Moorish portal of the Deliverance of Peter. Archi-

volts, though so tiny, are delicately molded, as in actual structures of the period. The impost blocks of these capitals are the most remarkable in the cloister; they include rare figure motifs drawn from foreign art, like the dog or wolf-headed men and the putti in scrolls, and plant forms unknown elsewhere in the cloister. Details like the hair and beard, which retain the patterned dispositions of the other capitals and the piers, are more plastically rendered (Fig. 89). In the discussion of design and space the slightly more complex groupings of this master have already been noted. If the sculptor of the north gallery in his most developed work employs undercutting and detaches limbs from the background, he never models folds even as slightly as this artist, nor chisels underneath the ends of drapery to lift them from the surface behind.

Fig. 90. Cloister; Capital of South Gallery: The Vision of John—the Angel with the Sickle

Fig. 91.
Cloister; Capital
of North Gal-
lery: The Angel
Gabriel

THE MASTERS OF THE CLOISTER

In the discussion of the pier reliefs I inquired if there were any evidences of change of style during the course of a long enterprise. It was observed that proportions vary from a squat to a taller canon and that certain refinements of detail visible in some figures are absent from others. But it was impossible to affirm with certainty that these differences mark a development. For they are not coordinated, but sporadic; and the more sophisticated or skilled forms appear side by side with others of more archaic character. Yet even these variations are significant. They indicate at least one source of new forms in the striving to individualize figures that are identical in decorative function and architectural position and belong to the same iconographic program; and another source in the greater skill and assuredness that results from a long

project in which the same problem—an almost life-size figure—is undertaken at least ten times.

The figure of Simon (Figs. 25, 27) seemed sufficiently unlike the others to provoke inquiry into the possibility of an independent authorship. His head at first sight appears uglier than the others. His jaw has a pronounced salience; the lips are pursed in a novel manner, while the three-quarters turn of the head is a boldness unparalleled in any of the apostles. Other details confirm the difference. No eyes are so large as Simon's; none but Peter and Paul (Figs. 28, 29) possess a similarly incised iris. In Peter and Paul, the incision is less prominent. The draperies of this exceptional apostle repeat the forms of the others, but in a more insistent and schematic manner. Almost the entire surface of his body is spun with closely grouped concentric and parallel lines. The curves have a uniform waviness less accentuated in the others. The fold of the left knee is thick, prominent, and unexpected. Likewise, the lower curve of the abdominal ellipse, common to most of the figures of the cloister, is raised in an unusual relief. Simon is further remarkable as the one apostle who copies closely the forms of another. We have only to compare him with the figure of Matthew (Fig. 22) to realize that they are not the works of the same hand. The open inscribed book of Matthew has some significance in the portrait of an evangelist; the inscription reproduces the initials of the opening words of his gospel. But in the representation of Simon such an open inscribed book departs from the traditional iconography and implies a confusion of types. The script of Simon's text (CANANEUS) is coarser than Matthew's; in accord with the accentuation of the repeated lines of the garment, the ruled lines of the book, omitted in the book of Matthew, are here incised.

A single detail confirms the notion of a separate authorship of the figure of Simon. It is the design of the capitals of his columnar frame. These are unique among all the capitals represented on the pier reliefs in the zigzag line connecting the volutes, as on the historiated capitals of the cloister. They are unique also in that the two capitals are unlike and that their ornament includes motifs found on none of the other piers. One is a central palmette flanked by large acanthus leaves which emerge from its lower lobes. This ornament appears on imposts of the cloister as well as on a capital of the east gallery.

The relief of Simon is not very distinct from the others. The differences are perceptible in small de-tails and in that general effect of a whole figure, which is difficult to define except by minute comparisons. Simon is more restless than his fellows. He is not firmly planted on the ground but is weighted on the toes. The symmetrical bending of the knees contributes to this effect of impermanence and expectancy in his position.

In the capitals of the cloister a broad distinction of styles has already been indicated in the contrast of the drapery forms, as well as in the differences in design and representation; but a more precise distinction of individual hands among all the sculptures of the cloister is difficult to establish because of the variations within any group and the unique effect produced in certain of the subjects. Since work continued for a considerable time, the development of the style and a possible mutual influence of the sculptors upon each other might account for the variety observed.

In the south gallery, however, the ten eastern capitals form a homogeneous group with peculiarities of drapery form, technique, ornament, and design that appear in no other capitals. This was apparent throughout the discussion of the style of the cloister sculptures. The master of these capitals is not the author of the pier reliefs, for although conventions of the latter are still employed by him, his own unusual forms are unknown on the piers. Which capitals were carved by the pier master is not certain because all the other capitals reproduce his forms. But they do this with varying skill and artistic result, so that several hands may be inferred. I believe that among the un-

Fig. 92. Cloister; Capital of South Gallery: Stephen Preaching

Fig. 93. Cloister; Capital of West Gallery: The Offering of Cain

Fig. 94.
Cloister; Capital
at Corner of
East Gallery:
Samson and the
Lion

Fig. 95.
Cloister; Capital
of North Gal-
lery: The Three
Hebrews in the
Fiery Furnace

engaged capitals of the north gallery and in a few of the west and south may be identified the works of the pier master. Those of the west are the Angels bearing the Cross (Fig. 44), the Beatitudes (Fig. 82), the Ascension of Alexander, Cain and Abel (Fig. 93); of the south, Nebuchadnezzar (Figs. 47, 74), Babylon, and the Martyrdom of Stephen (Figs. 48, 92). With these may be included most of the adjoining capitals with animal, plant, and figure ornament.

In the capitals listed may be observed all the details of the piers rendered with identical precision, though they are of a different scale. Especially in the north gallery, a figure like the Christ calling the apostles

(Fig. 50) is evidently of the same artistic family as the apostles on the piers. The fine surface finish of these capitals also distinguishes them from the closely related capitals engaged to the pier and from those of the east gallery. In the capitals of the pier master little or no addition is made to the repertoire of drapery forms used on the piers, other than the banding of the torso and those elements which belong to contemporary dress. His themes are broadly spaced and clear, the movements of the figures restrained, their bodies more rounded, and the details more sharply cut than on the capitals engaged to the piers, or in the east gallery. A comparison of the Three Hebrews in the

Fig. 96.
Cloister; Capital
of East Gallery:
Martyrdom of
St. Laurence

Furnace (Fig. 95) with the analogous Spanish saints in the east gallery (Fig. 83), and of Daniel between the lions in the north gallery (Fig. 69) with the more archaic Daniel by another master in the west (Fig. 86), will establish these characteristics of the master. They are reflected in the inscriptions, which are placed on the horizontal bands of the impost or, if cut within the capital itself, are more clearly and regularly aligned than in the east gallery. On the capital of Martin dividing his cloak an inscription is incised on the sword (Fig. 54). But there are at least two, if not more, alphabets on the capitals of this group. The inscriptions were added by different hands: or the single sculptor possessed the versatility and habit of scribes who in the books of the period composed titles and headings in several manners.[95] The resemblance of the figures on the capital of the Three Hebrews to those on the capital of Benedict and Martin is so great that the remarkable difference in their inscriptions cannot be a criterion of different authorship of the capitals.

Two capitals in the west gallery—with the Raising of Lazarus (Fig. 70) and the Anointing of David (Fig.

85)—might be early works of the pier master. They are somewhat cruder in finish and simpler in design than the capitals of the north gallery but have very similar shapes. They point also to the capitals engaged to the piers (Figs. 76, 94) which, though by one hand, display a variety that indicates a developing style.

Related to the engaged capitals are those of the east gallery and the Shepherds in the south (Fig. 32), which present a distinct epigraphic style, with larger, more angular letters than the south or north capitals. But the Shepherds and some sculptures in the east gallery—the Washing of Feet (Fig. 75), Lazarus and Dives (Figs. 67, 68), Cana (Figs. 30, 52), the Magi (Figs. 35, 36, 37), and the three Spanish saints (Figs. 33, 77, 83, 97)—are so much more archaic in the canon of the figure, the large head and squat body, the compact compositions, the heavy folds, and extremely schematic forms that one must ask if they are not the works of a fourth hand. Similar figures exist beside the more usual type on engaged capitals (Baptism, Fig. 76). Even in the works of the pier master and the south gallery there is a similar range in proportions and style of drapery. The more archaic works may be earlier carvings of the sculptor who did the other capitals of the east gallery and the engaged columns. One fact, however, seems to point to a distinct authorship of this more archaic group. The letters of the inscriptions are not uniformly aligned but strewn in diagonals and verticals on the surface of the capital between the figures. The eight engaged capitals are uninscribed except for the SAMSON which is placed, not on the field of sculpture, but on the console above it. The decomposed diagonal inscriptions occur on the Shepherds, the Martyrdom of the Three Spanish Saints, and Peter and Paul (Fig. 87), as well as on the five capitals listed above. The figure of the king in the Martyrdom of Saturninus (Fig. 43) appears to be by the same hand as Herod in the Massacre (Fig. 35) and Emilianus in the three Spanish Saints (Fig. 97), and Saul on the engaged capital of David and Goliath. Within this large group of the eastern gallery and the engaged capitals there is a stylistic span in which I have perhaps failed to distinguish two or even three different hands. I am still uncertain whether the pier capitals are to be grouped with those of the east gallery, or whether the Adam and Eve (Figs. 34, 39, 40) and the Martyrdom of Laurence (Figs. 57, 96) belong with the others. The identity of the nude figures of Adam and Eve with the nude souls of Peter and Paul points to a common authorship. But other details of these two capitals are less obviously similar.

The capitals engaged to the piers might be considered the works of the pier master, were it not that the forms used by the sculptor of the north and west galleries are even closer to those of the apostles, and that common novelties like the lifted mantle of the high priest in the Miracle of Peter and a figure at the Feast of Herod (Fig. 2) are more neatly and skillfully rendered in the first than in the second. Besides, on the pier capitals occur several details of drapery, chevron incisions, zigzag ends, and flying folds of a heavy flattened character unknown in either the pier reliefs or the capitals of the north gallery, and far less developed than in the south.

The intrusion in the west gallery of a capital like the Shepherds may be explained in the light of two of its peculiarities. It is of greater width, by four centimeters, than any other capital of this gallery. It received not only the weight of the gallery arches but also of the bay of the lavatorium arcade which began at this point, and has left traces of its haunch and spring above the impost of this capital. Hence it may be supposed that this capital belongs to another mo-

ment in the architectural enterprise, being either a slightly earlier reemployed capital or the work of a hand introduced in the course of this new construction. A similar departure from the normal width of the capitals occurs in the Washing of Feet (Fig. 75), a capital of a more friable material than the others, and with unusually compact figures and simple, forceful execution.

To which of the masters of the cloister the figure of Simon (Fig. 27) is due I cannot decide. It is surely not the work of the sculptor of the south gallery, but in the remaining capitals there are no figures sufficiently like Simon to suggest a common hand. A little head projecting from the tower beside Nero in the Martyrdom of Peter and Paul (Fig. 87) has a similar appearance. The other figures of this capital, however, are distinct from the apostle. The existence of a capital in the east gallery with the exceptional foliate forms of the relief of Simon also points to one of the hands of the east gallery.

In the cloister the evident differences between the capitals of the east gallery and those of the south are not due to an internal development during the course of work, or even to a gradual transformation of the first style during a longer time. The two groups are contemporary, and even the stylistically intermediate group of the pier master (north gallery) is of the same period. I should not say "intermediate," for this word presupposes a logical or historical order of development which is contradicted by closer observation. For if the capitals of the north gallery (B) are more refined and more naturalistic than those of the east (A), and less developed in drapery forms and ornament than the capitals of the south (C), their compositions and space are as complex as C's, and their inscrip-

Fig. 97. Cloister; Capital of East Gallery: Martyrdom of the Three Spanish Saints—the Prefect Emilianus

tions, in fact, more modern. Noteworthy is the presence on the crudest capitals in the east gallery of the zigzag folds and projecting ends of drapery, unknown in B. In the possession of these forms the most archaic capitals intimate a subsequent development, unannounced in B. It may be, however, that they are copied from the style of C, and that far from being an antecedent of C, the capitals of A are an adaptation of C to an earlier manner. But this seems unlikely to me because of the specific character of the broken draperies in A; they presuppose only the simpler pleatings of C and show no trace of the more developed forms even in a coarsened or reduced version.

If we observe within a given group certain variations from one capital to another, they may be interpreted as the stages of a personal development. But these variations within a group are less radical than the differences between the groups as wholes. We can infer a common preoccupation with more naturalistic forms, but it would not account for the striking stylistic differences between the groups and the presence of divergent stylistic tendencies. In the north gallery the draperies are rarely the source of expression or movement; we find more animated draperies and episodic lively compositions in the eastern capitals, which are, however, the most remote from the south gallery in design and naturalism. In the latter, the most novel forms, even if associated with a more complex whole and more complex details, do not imply a uniform transformation of every feature of an earlier practice. Those forms which promote linear movement and intensified peripheral rhythms along the contours are the most radically developed; side by side with the more elongated and naturalistic figures and the finer draperies persist the primitive conventions of stance and the most marked deformations. The feet are still separated at a straight angle or are suspended vertically without support, while the earlier fractioned representation of parts appears in such enormities as the right arm of the demon who embraces Christ in the scene of the Temptation (Fig. 84). It is as long as his own body from head to foot. In this group the change of style appears at first as the result of a simple addition of new motifs to the common stock of forms rather than in a central quality that pervasively modifies every detail from within. The old are not completely modified by the intrusive combinations, but exist beside them in the very same figures. This is evident in some imposts where the common palmette acquires a more plastic character in the south gallery by the simple ridging or curling of a lobe, or by the sheathing of a stem, the plant other-

wise remaining the same. But beside this gradual change, which reflects a plastic tendency in the complication of surfaces and also a search for more intricate and more numerous lines, we recognize the novel motifs of ornament employed by the same sculptor beside the slightly altered palmette. Their richness corresponds to the complexity imposed on the latter; they include in another context the ridging, sheathing, and curling introduced in the palmette. We are led to suppose that the larger change in the common types is not simply an internal development but has been produced by the intrusion or observation of another style. What forms resulted from the more self-contained development of the original types can be seen in the north gallery, which lacks precisely the novel drapery forms and rich surfaces of the south, although it often goes beyond the latter in the naturalistic postures, proportions, and design of the figures.

The masters of the south and east galleries (especially of the Wedding of Cana and the Washing of Feet), though contemporary, represent nonetheless two poles of a development within the local Romanesque art. In the second we observe in the clearest manner, on capitals of more massive, almost rectangular block form, a style of compact, immobile figures, grouped in ornamental sequences or antithetic schemes, as simple as the structure of the figures themselves. The contours and surfaces of these squat, bulging figures are often only slightly differentiated; they are conceived descriptively as a naively realistic, itemized composition of isolated, geometrically formed parts. In the south gallery, on the other hand, an effect of freer movement is achieved by a proliferation of radial and meandering lines of drapery, by taller, more slender figures with an increased flexibility of posture, by asymmetrical, open compositions and a higher differentiation of surfaces, whereby the originally inert volumes, attached to the wall, are converted into slightly more articulated, more plastic structures that suggest an incipient liberation from the background in an implied if inconsistently framed space. Beside this artist, the other appears to be a carver of ornamental capitals of birds, beasts, and plants, who is also called upon to execute figured groups; while the first seems primarily a figure sculptor, who imposes on the ornamental portions of the capitals the individualized complexity of living objects. His astragals are not merely ornamented; they become representations of jeweled, banded, cordlike objects. In his series of ten capitals, unlike those by the other masters, there is not one purely decorative sculpture. But his progressive naturalism goes hand in hand with the disengagement of line from a primitive inert massiveness and a simplified descriptive usage in a composition of discrete elements. Thus the two opposed characterizations of Romanesque style—as of architectonic, rigorously coordinated, weighty, symmetrical, culminating masses, and as a less plastic system of multiplied, contrasted lines—may both be verified in the sculptures of the cloister. But in the capitals of the south gallery, this second character, already evident within the most archaic capitals, is intensified, and anticipates the later tympanum of Moissac.

It is important to observe that at the very beginning of the modern tradition of sculpture there is already great freedom and divergence from a common method in the same project, and that the variations are not uniformly directed. This freedom corresponds to the variety of subject matter and the motifs of ornament, unlike the stereotypes and limited range in other traditions. The basic unity of the whole is apparent when we compare it with works of another region, like Burgundy. The uniform structure of the capitals is its clearest expression.

A NOTE ON TECHNIQUE

There are no capitals in an unfinished state at Moissac which would permit us to study the method of carving. Hence it must be inferred from the completed works and by comparison with contemporaneous unfinished capitals in the same region. Luckily such a capital, from the cloister of the cathedral of Saint-Étienne, is preserved in the Musée des Augustins at Toulouse. It shows four figures blocked out and partially modeled, probably intended to represent the foolish virgins, since the wise virgins have been carved on the other side. The cutting is sufficiently advanced to enable us to judge the composition of the figures, their relative mass, the directions of the main lines, and the gestures. But no features are visible. The heads are simple eggs, the hair, broad unstriated surfaces in high relief. It is remarkable that the shoes have been carried further than other parts of the figures, perhaps because of their simple shape. It may be supposed from this capital that at Moissac the sculptor drew upon the smoothed block of the stone the broad outlines of the figures and cut away the intervals between them to establish their full salience. The figure was not completed part by part, but, as far as can be judged from this capital in Toulouse and another in the Archaeological Museum of Nev-

ers, the capital was chiseled as a whole, stage by stage, except for the final details. The background was smoothed early in the work. In this method are implied a clear contrast of salient masses and hollows and a preconception of the capital as a decorative, plastic whole.

The sculptor employed chisels and drills. I have observed no traces of a saw in Moissac and Toulouse, as in the earliest Greek sculptures. The forms of the chisels are difficult to determine, since the finished surfaces of the capitals have been smoothed with a finer tool. But it is evident from the capital in Toulouse that a broad-edged chisel was employed in the preliminary (really the actual) labor, since the planes demarcated in the rough-hewn figures are so broad and sharply cut. Besides the chisels, pointed instruments must have been used; several kinds of delicate and coarse grooving, striation, and incision are visible. Some of these may have been accomplished with a narrow chisel, some with a gouge. The drill had a limited application. Traces of its use appear mainly in the ornament and in the cutting of apertures in the buildings rendered on the capitals. Unlike the sculptors of Cuxa, Elne, and the eastern part of Languedoc who retained the late classic practice of drilling details of eyes, mouth, and other parts of the body, the atelier of Moissac employed the drill to represent hollows of circular section. It is possible, however, that it was applied also in undercutting of heads and limbs of some of the figures and animals. Such undercutting is exceptional in the cloister, but more common in later works of the region. The practice of undercutting is evidenced in the missing parts of figures, in the loss of heads and limbs that left no scar on the background from which they were in part detached. On the capitals of the south gallery, the contours of drapery are in places lifted slightly from the background, and the heads in high relief, while not free from the wall, touch it at only a single point.

The effect of the various materials—the marble and limestone—upon the sculptor's labor and conceptions is beyond my competence to judge. It is incorrect to reason as does Monsieur Rey[96] that the "progress" of Romanesque sculpture follows the substitution of white calcareous stone for marble, which is less easy to cut, or that the archaism of certain sculptures is simply the result of refractory materials. He cites early Greek sculpture as an example of the consequences of different materials, "poros" and marble, on style. Yet in Greece it is precisely the softer poros which preceded the marble. Had he observed more closely the sculptures of Moissac, of which he has written, he would have seen that in the same calcareous stone is carved a great diversity of figures and that the few marble imposts are neither more nor less crudely decorated than the simple limestone. Not only the most primitive capitals in the cloister (the Shepherds, Cana, Washing of Feet) are in the latter material, but also the most highly developed in design, realism, technique, and complexity of ornament—those of the south gallery. The marble pier reliefs stand between them; but on the later porch the most delicate carving appears on the marble reliefs of the Visitation and Unchastity.

For many years it has been asked whether Romanesque capitals were carved in place, from the scaffolding, or in the workshop prior to elevation on the column. For the conditions of labor are manifestly different in the two methods. In the first the sculptor is not as free to manipulate the capital. In the second, however, he lacks the direct vision of its relation to the column, walls, and adjacent moldings. According to most students, Gothic sculptures were all carved in the atelier and set in the walls and arches afterwards, while in the Romanesque period both practices are observable. Labor on the scaffold supposedly explains the lack of delicacy in some Romanesque works. Placed high above the ground the sculptor had less ease and assurance in his labor and undertook fewer refinements. This, however, is uncertain, for a skillful sculptor, accustomed to scaffold conditions, was less limited by them. What is called crude is sometimes a willful simplification, or an early work of a powerful plastic sensibility. The inference of sculpture *après* and *avant la pose* is made from the relation of the carving to the wall in which it is fitted. If a capital engaged to a wall is carved on all its sides despite its partial concealment, it is apparently an atelier rather than scaffold product. But the perfectly adapted capital may as well be an atelier as a scaffold sculpture, for the specifications and context could have been readily anticipated. The determination of the method has more often been a subject of controversies over dating rather than of strict technical inquiry. To justify dating of sculptures later than the known consecration or completion of the building, it has been argued that the capitals were carved long after they had been set up rough-hewn on the columns; while those who defended a precocious dating of sculptures in a building constructed over a long period of years invoked the theory of a sculpture *avant la pose* to corroborate an attribution to a time when construction had barely started.

In Moissac the capitals are on columns so low that a scaffolding was probably never employed. On the capital of the Annunciation engaged to the northeast pier (Fig. 31), the servant is cut at the left in order to fit the vertical surface of the pier. This would not have happened if the capital had been carved *in situ*, for then the sculptor would have adapted the figure to the narrow space. It is possible, on the other hand, that this cutting is due to the later reconstruction in the thirteenth century when the pointed arches were erected. Vöge[97] supposed that the earliest Romanesque sculptures, and especially those of southern France, were carved in place, but there are several capitals in Toulouse, on the portals of St.-Sernin and of St. Pierre-des-Cuisines (a priory of Moissac), of which the faces turned to the jambs are sculptured like the others. They were therefore carved before their erection on the columns. It is certain also that the earliest capitals of the cloister of Silos, which date from the end of the eleventh century, were not carved in place, since in the clusters of five capitals at the midpoints of the arcades the central capital is as minutely carved as the others, although hardly accessible to a chisel between the four supporting columns.

THE SCULPTURES OF THE SOUTH PORTAL AND PORCH

II

THE TYMPANUM

The first Romanesque art of Moissac appears in numerous capitals, some decorated with religious subjects. Larger reliefs are of single figures. The whole recalls an illuminated Bible in which the miniatures of each book are preceded by a full-page figure of the author. Initials are fancifully wrought with beasts and flowers as on some of the capitals.

In the tympanum of the south portal (Figs. 98, 99) the sculpture of Moissac becomes truly monumental. It is placed above the level of the eye, and is so large as to dominate the entire entrance. It is a gigantic semi-circular relief, five meters and sixty-eight centimeters in diameter, framed by a slightly pointed archivolt in three orders. Its great mass is supported by a magnificently ornamented lintel, a sculptured trumeau, and two doorposts of cusped profile, on which are carved figures of Peter and the prophet Isaiah. The portal is sheltered by a salient barrel-vaulted porch, decorated on its lower inner walls with reliefs representing incidents from the Infancy of Christ, the story of Lazarus and Dives, and the Punishment of Avarice and Unchastity. On the exterior of this porch, which is attached to the south wall of the western tower of the church, the figures of the abbot Roger (1115–1131) and St. Benedict (?) have been set above engaged columns.

In its grouping and concentration of sculpture the porch is comparable in enterprise to an arch of triumph. The tympanum alone is a work of architecture, for twenty-eight blocks of stone were brought together to form its surface. That so shortly after the reemergence of figure carving in stone such great monuments were attempted testifies to the rapidity of development and the unhampered ambitions of monastic builders in the presence of new means and new powers.

On the tympanum, about a central group of a gigantic crowned Christ enthroned in majesty with the four symbols of the evangelists and two seraphim, are placed the four-and-twenty elders bearing chalices and various stringed instruments (Figs. 99–118). These verses of the fourth and fifth chapters of the Apocalyptic vision of John are almost literally rendered:

Revelations iv, 2 . . . and behold, a throne was set in heaven, and one sat on the throne.

3. And he that sat was to look upon like a jasper and a sardine stone; and there was a rainbow round about the throne, in sight like to an emerald.

4. And round about the throne were four and twenty seats; and upon the seats I saw four and twenty elders sitting, clothed in white raiment; and they had on their heads crowns of gold.

Church: East Wall of Porch: The Annunciation to Joseph, Detail of Fig. 120

Fig. 98.
Church: South
Porch of Narthex

6. And before the throne there was a sea of glass like unto crystal: and in the midst of the throne, and round about the throne, were four beasts full of eyes before and behind.

7. And the first beast was like a lion, and the second beast like a calf, and the third beast had a face as a man, and the fourth beast was like a flying eagle.

v, 1. And I saw in the right hand of him that sat on the throne a book written within and on the back side, sealed with seven seals.

8. . . . and four and twenty elders . . . , having every one of them harps, and golden vials full of odors, which are the prayers of the saints.

The tympanum does not render a specific line of the Apocalyptic text but a characteristic and impressive moment of the vision. It omits the "lightnings and thunderings and voices" and the "seven lamps of fire burning before the throne"; and though the elders are given instruments and phials, they do not kneel before the lamb, as in the verse which describes them, "having every one of them harps and golden vials full of odors, which are the prayers of the saints." The two angels with scrolls are likewise abstracted from their immediate context (Rev. v, 2, mentions one angel, and v, 11, "ten thousand times ten thousand, and thousands of thousands"), and with their six wings are the seraphim of Isaiah's vision (Isaiah vi, 2), not John's. Unlike the text of Revelation, Christ blesses with his right hand and holds the sealed book in his left, while the four beasts, whose evangelistic symbolism is absent from John, are given the books a later tradition ascribed to them. The crown and cross nimbus of Christ are also additions to the original vision. The symbols have not the six wings or the many eyes a literal rendering would demand (Rev. iv, 8), but only two wings, in departure from both John and Ezekiel. Their arrangement about the throne follows the order of the heads of Ezekiel's tetramorph rather than the text of John.

With all these modifications of the vision, the tympanum is yet wonderfully in accord with it. A simple hierarchical conception of the Apocalyptic numbers is expressed in its design. The central and largest figure is the one God; next in magnitude are the two seraphim; then follow the four symbolic beasts; and smallest and most removed from Christ are the twenty-four elders in three rows. The symbolic beauty of this conception, which is unique in the iconography of the theme, will be apparent from a confrontation with some ancient traditional version like the great mosaic of St. Paul's in Rome.[98] Here only the bust of Christ is represented in a large medallion, above tiny angels; the symbols fly in a vast heaven beside him, while the elders, grouped in two unequal rows of twelve, are tall figures, as large as the object of their veneration.

Beside this theological contrast of magnitude and number, the abstract elements of design, the symmetry, and the proliferation of energetically opposed animated lines reinforce the vision, and the numerous details of terrestrial ornament and distinctions, unmentioned in the text, contribute to the reality of heavenly splendor. The meander ribbon, issuing from the jaws of monsters, bounds the whole vision and is lost under the wings of the seraphim and symbols, like the heaven of a primitive cosmogony.

The attribution of repose to only one figure in the whole tympanum, the seated Christ, who is placed in the center of the field, and the surrounding of this dominating center with large figures in energetic movement, are conceived in the spirit of Apocalyptic imagery. The directing of the heads of the numerous little elders toward the central figure of Christ produces an effect of peripheral waves reaching out to the corners of the tympanum. Ten of the elders sit with legs crossed; the others acquire a similar animation by the contrasts of limbs and instruments. The wavy lines of the sea of glass, the meandering ribbon under the archivolt, and the dense, serried feathers of the many wings contribute further to the restlessness of the whole. The focus is maintained throughout, and all the details seem to revolve about Christ. Even the sea of glass halts for a moment before his feet; the amplitude of the wave is noticeably greater here in acknowledgment of the common center.

The thirty-one figures are distributed symmetrically in contrasting directions. In the center is the vertical Christ; around him the circle of symbolic beasts flanked by the two seraphim; and beside and below them, in horizontal bands, are the seated elders. The zoning of the latter parallels the lintel so that the frieze of rosettes seems a part of the figure composition, and a great cross is thereby created of the vertical Christ and the trumeau, and these bands of elders and the lintel. The side doorposts further prolong the verticals of the seraphim and oppose the horizontal bands above by their contrasting divisions; while their scalloped contours flank the trumeau just as the similar curves of the symbols accost the central figure of Christ.

This architectural composition is stressed by the distinct isolation of all the elements. The elders are grouped as separate individuals in clear alignment. The encroachment of one figure on another is only peripheral and never obscures the second. The high relief of the wavy borders of the horizontal zones provides a definite boundary of the groups of elders; and the difference of scale between Christ, the symbols, and the seraphim creates an equally effective segregation.

The distribution of the figures and the zoning of groups of elders do not correspond strictly to any underlying architectural divisions. The appearance of molded frames between the bands of elders is a sculptured contrivance rather than an actual jointing. Likewise, the central group of Christ and the symbols is independent of the structure of the tympanum and is composed on several slabs on which figures have been carved without much attention to the joints. It was inevitable that these should to some extent correspond to the figures, but the latter are not determined by them. Whatever appearance of architectonic order the tympanum produces is the result of an independent design which has a decorative regularity and a symmetry to a large extent self-evolved. This conception of tympanum design must be distinguished from that of Chartres and of Gothic portals, in which each group corresponds to an architectural division of the registers of the lintel and the upper lunette. It accords with the latter only insofar as the use of numerous slabs, as in a mosaic composition, imposed some sys-

tem or economy on the sculptor and demanded that he avoid as far as possible the extension of one figure on two slabs. Hence the smaller elders are carved singly or in groups of two on single blocks of stone; but the larger Christ and the adjoining figures are cut by the joints of several slabs. Compare this with Chartres where each voussoir has its own figure or complete ornament and the main figures of the tympana, like Christ and the Virgin, are carved on single blocks of stone.

Within the symmetrical design and simple arrangement of its numerous parts, the tympanum includes irregularities which are manifestly planned, but not apparent without close examination. These irregularities are not the small variations inevitable in human workmanship, to which in reaction against the machine one attributes an inherent aesthetic worth, but decided deviations from an expected sequence or a canonical geometric form. They produce expressive contrasts and exciting interruptions in accord with the restless animation of the tympanum as a whole. Thus the repeated wavy lines below the upper-most band of elders are not only discontinuous; they are not strictly parallel. The even number of figures on the lowest zone and the symmetry of the whole tympanum precluded an elder directly beneath Christ. Such a figure would have detracted from the exclusive centrality of the latter and given too great a prominence to the vertical axis in a primarily radial and concentric scheme. Yet the sculptor, with a fine feeling for the exigency of the design, and in avoidance of a static precision, has arranged the heads of the elders beneath Christ in an asymmetrical series, so that one is nearer to the axis than the other (Figs. 99, 100). The parallel rather than divergent diagonals of the instruments confirm this asymmetry and produce a contrast of directions within the group of four.

This deviation from the expected symmetry is as artfully sustained in the lintel, where there is likewise no single central unit but a juncture of rosettes at a point to the left of the axis of the tympanum and the central division of the row of elders. The slight preponderance of the right side of the lintel is perhaps designed to balance the arm of Christ extended at the left. But the shifting of the axes is a corollary of a more general movement in the design of the whole.

Just as the ten rosettes are not aligned with equal intervals, the heads of the elders show a similar casualness in their arrangement, which appears rhythmical and necessary when more closely observed. If we number as 1 to 8 (from left to right) the separate slabs on which the lower zone of elders is carved, we see that the head of the inner figure of 4 is farther from the axis than the opposed head on 5; and in consequence the interval between the two heads on 4 is less than on 5; the inner head of 3 is, in contrasting interval, farther from the axis than the corresponding head on 6, and its distance from its mate is less than in 6. On each side there is one interposition of a chalice in a wide interval. But these two chalices are

Fig. 99.
Church: Tym-panum of South Porch

Fig. 100.
Church; Detail of Tympanum: Elders of Bottom Row

Fig. 101.
Church; Detail of Tympanum: Christ and the Symbols

not symmetrical; one is in the extreme left block, the other in the fifth, near the center of the whole zone. If the bosses of the heads are considered single plastic units of equal magnitude and salience, and the chalices, minor masses, then the pattern of bump and hollow is hardly as regular as the general orderliness of the tympanum would lead us to expect. On the zone above there are two groups of three elders (Figs. 99, 102, 103). On the left they are arranged: two, large interval, one; on the right the three are separated by two large intervals.

In the symmetrical central group of Christ, the symbols, and the seraphim the dynamic character of the coordination is especially apparent. The seven heads form an elliptical figure of horizontal major axis in contrast to the dominant vertical Christ and in closer accord with the shape of the tympanum. The wings of the lion have been turned upward to connect his head with the left seraph, a modification of the symmetry of the two lower beasts, which adds wonderfully to their energetic movement. In contrast to the flexed arm of the left seraph, the left arm of the other seraph is designed to complete the ellipse of the heads. The implied figure is not really an ellipse, but a less regular form, since the heads of the seraphim

are nearer to the upper than to the lower symbols. The bull's head is higher than the lion's, the eagle's higher than the man's, and in consequence these four heads determine diagonal, not vertical or horizontal lines. The glances of the lower beasts are not directed toward Christ, but in powerful intensification of the movement of the geometrically ordered tympanum trace a great X with the crossing point beneath the convergent symmetrical beard of Christ. There is an obvious multiplication of parallel diagonals, like the horns and wing of the bull and the wavy lines on his back, which accent the same intersecting scheme. It is further complicated by the diagonal draperies on the body of Christ.

Even Christ (Fig. 101), the one strictly frontal figure on the tympanum, is asymmetrical in the benedictional gesture of his raised right hand, in the contrasting arrangement of the folds of the two shoulders, and in the great sweep of drapery at the left ankle, unduplicated on the right. This drapery is the immediate counterpart of the arched back of the bull, from which it seems to diverge, and opposes in its curve the right arm of Christ and the enveloping folds. By means of these diagonally contrasted elements, the figure of Christ, though solidly enthroned, acquires some of the animation of the surrounding forms. There is also an element of strain or inner tension due to the sloping thighs and legs, which form a zigzag line with the diverging feet. The inclined throne, as a plane diagonal to the common wall, is a corresponding motif in relief.

How deliberately such forms were sought and turned to the common end appears in the tail of the bull (Fig. 114), which sweeps upward with the lower edge of Christ's robe and with the long fold that issues from under the jeweled edge of the mantle (and also with the bull's hind leg and his back, and even the sea of glass) and then suddenly drops, diverging in four radial, curved locks, like the fan-shaped folds to the left. The lion's tail describes an analogous curve; but the symmetry of these tails is disturbed by the rhythmical opposition of the ends, the one pointing upward, the other down (Fig. 113). Such intensity of linear design is sustained throughout, and collaborates with oppositions of relief to stir the more rigid geometrical framework of the whole. We have only to examine a small portion of relief, like the hind leg and flank of the lion, to perceive the excited, vigorous movement of the well-ordered forms. The symmetry and zoning appear for a moment as elements of the vision, or simple devices of order in architectural design, rather than an essential pervasive scheme.

Fig. 106.
Church; Detail
of Tympanum:
Elder of Bottom
Row

Fig. 107.
Church, Detail
of Tympanum:
Elder of Bottom
Row

It is characteristic of the style that the individual figures cannot be reduced to a banded or symmetrical design like the tympanum itself. This is sufficiently clear in the animals, in the symbol of Matthew, and in the elongated zigzag postures of the seraphim. Even the smaller elders are as complex in design. Though the heads are fixed on a common point, the bodies have a wonderfully varied and independent life which maintains the movement of the tympanum in every block. There are no two elders who sit alike or whose garments are similarly arranged. The patterned zigzags of falling draperies are continually varied and attest to the ingenious fancy of the sculptor. The heads, also, show this in their tilted poses, in the diversity of hair, beards, and crowns. The instruments and chalices furnish additional motifs capable of as great variety though similarly shaped; raised or lowered, held horizontally or diagonally, in the right or left hand, they form essential parts of unique conceptions of each figure. Those who are seated at the outer edge and touch upon the archivolt have an additional source of rhythmic complexity in a thick ribbon framing the tympanum. Its irregular beaded meander is in lower relief than the figures which at times overlap it, but it moves with them and their

sharp angles of limb and instrument are contrived to parallel its winding form.

A study of the two elders seated opposite each other in the upper zone adjoining the seraphim (Figs. 102, 103) will reveal much of the sculptor's intention and his method of design. They are symmetrical with respect to the figure of Christ and are unusual among the figures of the tympanum in that their postures are so similar despite the constant variation of the corresponding units of the two sides of the relief. They are seated in repose, with the right leg placed across the left in an impossible horizontality. In both figures the left leg is perfectly straight, in evident architectural contrast to the supported limb. This post and lintel construction is maintained by the vertical instruments of the two elders, and by the lines of the torsos and draperies. The arms too preserve as straight a line as possible and, if slightly curved, do not cross the torso. The heads alone offer a prominent contrast to this rectangular scaffolding, for they are turned to the figure of Christ between them.

The repetition of the crossing of legs is an asymmetrical motif, for the same leg is crossed in the two figures, instead of the parts corresponding in a symmetrical composition. If both instruments are held

Fig. 108.
Church; Detail
of Tympanum:
Elder at Right
End of Lowest
Row

Fig. 109.
Church; Detail
of Tympanum:
Elder at Right
End of Middle
Row

stiffly vertical, one is suspended from the horizontal limb, the other is raised above it. The left figure bears a chalice in his left hand, the other elder, with his right, draws a bow across the erect viol. The right elder has a short beard that forms a broad fringe across his jaw; the left elder's beard is long and stringy, with locks falling upon the breast and shoulders. The crowns, too, are contrasted—round in the one, polygonal in the other. There are also effective differences in costume and the disposition of the folds which are apparent in the photographs and require little comment. I must mention, however, those apparently descriptive details of the two figures which reconcile these differences and attach the divergent forms to the common framework. Such are the curved lines of the mantle of the left elder, enclosing the banded folds of the breast, and the straight lines of the same garment falling from the right leg behind the suspended instrument. In the other figure the same function is fulfilled by the viol and the curved bow, now damaged, which produce a similar play of curves across the torso, and the vertical fall of drapery from the horizontal leg, accented by a jeweled border, in counterpart to the suspended instrument of the other figure. A close study of the movements of the figures, the wings, and the folds, which as representations of real objects are strange and quaintly elaborate, reveals in them an impassioned logicality of decorative directions. Each line reechoes or answers its neighbor, and the mutual interest of these figures in the vision is corroborated in the relation of their smallest lines.[99]

The symmetry of these two figures is restless, though they are not in motion and express no inner disturbance; their forms have been designed in sustained opposition. Even in those elders who are ostensibly moved by the vision of God and sit uneasily or cross their legs, the effect of animation is primarily an imaginative contrivance of the sculptor, and issues more from the fantastic but coordinated play of lines than from the observation of excited human movements in nature.

The *contrapposto* observed in several capitals of the cloister is raised to a higher power on the tympanum by the forceful contrast of more numerous elements. The wonderful elders seated at the edges of the tympanum will illustrate this clearly (Figs. 108, 109). In these figures the movement of the head toward Christ is opposed by the arms or legs, as if the whole figure did not participate in the vision and the eyes were suddenly distracted from another object. Yet by these opposed movements, the expressiveness of the tympanum is considerably heightened and the excite-

ment of the center transmitted to the corners. The gesture that binds the elders to Christ is in fact part of an independent zigzag or *contrapposto* scheme. In the lower right figure (Fig. 108) the arms and thighs are carried to the right in contrast to the head, but the instrument is raised in opposition to this movement and the left leg crossed with a similar intention. By a radical distortion of the ankle the right foot is turned to form a diagonal converging toward the left. The beard is prolonged as a braided band parallel to the viol, the left leg, and the right foot. This Romanesque *contrapposto* is distinguished from the spiral torsion of Renaissance art in that (among other things) the pliable parts of the body—the torso and neck—preserve an independent rigidity, the larger form is zigzag rather than curved, the opposed movements are usually in planes parallel to the background, and the contrasted elements are divided or terminated by intricate, winding, and broken lines. In the Romanesque works the balance is largely unplastic, linear. It is no equilibrium of masses but a balance of directions in a single plane which is not designed to effect an ultimate repose. Instead of a redistribution of masses by which the body is relaxed, the sculptor has designed a scheme of opposed movements by which the limbs are uniformly strained. In the two seraphim (Fig. 112) the parallel bending of the legs balances the turn of the head, but this balance is a tense, restless posture that cannot be maintained. The knees are strained and the legs fixed in a movement away from the rest of the figure. In the elder at the

*Fig. 110.
Church; Detail
of Tympanum:
the Left Seraph*

extreme right of the middle row (Fig. 109) the crossed feet form an unstable, unsupporting mass. In the corresponding figure on the left the instrument is suspended diagonally, outside the main body mass. Observe how even in such small details as the position of the hand grasping the chalice, the sculptor has sometimes chosen an arbitrary and difficult articulation. In the middle zone of the left side of the tympanum the second elder holds the cup suspended between two fingers, not at the base but at the upper bowl. The elder at the extreme right of the same zone has twisted his arm in order to grasp the chalice with the thumb outward.

On the tympanum the body is only one element in the equilibrium of the figure. It is part of a larger scheme in which the drapery and instruments have a considerable role. In the outer elder of the upper left zone the body is bent diagonally from left to right, and the draperies suspended from his left arm and the parallel instrument, now destroyed, maintain the balance of the figure (Fig. 102). But even with this coordination of lines the result is less a stabilized structure of parts than a restless crossing of lines. I have already mentioned the extended instruments of other elders (Fig. 108) which, in balancing the turn of the head and legs, create an additional strain. The very overlapping of the meandering ribbon by those figures (Figs. 108, 109) is a reflection of the same character of the style. Where such external lines do not enter to oppose or play with the body forms, the edges of the garment are broken in meandering pleats that produce a similar effect. The body is rarely isolated as a closed, self-balanced mass, but is usually a complex angular structure in a more intricate system of moving lines.

Even this dominant structure is subordinate to a linear surface design, despite its high relief and apparent plastic strength. There are numerous planes diagonal or perpendicular to the background, but they are limited to the individual figures and are never prolonged to modify the spatial form of the whole. They are not conceived as directions proceeding from the outer surface of the tympanum toward the background, but as the indispensable outward projection of a figure placed against a wall. We shall grasp this character of the figure more clearly when we have examined the space of the tympanum as a whole.

The Apocalyptic vision is rendered on the tympanum rather than in it. The space of the literary conception is compressed into the architectural limits defined by the enclosing arch of the relief and the impenetrable Romanesque wall. The sculptor does

not attempt to suggest an expanse wider than the portal or deeper than the thickness of the stone. If the elders and symbols circle about Christ, it is in one plane; they can step neither behind nor before him.[100] They are on the stones placed above or beside, none more salient than the other, to form a sculptured wall.

This archaic equality of projection is essential to the formal unity and the architectural setting, and is hardly perceived as a contradiction of the vision. Yet, just as the symmetry of the whole includes so great asymmetry in the members, the apparently flat surface composition unites figures that are all so deeply cut as to constitute separate free statues in the round. Regarded from the side, the elders seem an array of men seated on a narrow ledge, rather than applied or engraved upon a wall. The heads of some of them are even detached from the background, the necks undercut, and the arms and instruments free, except at one or two points. This new boldness in carving accounts in part for the destruction of projecting members and accessories.

But the contrast of figure and neutral background is so regular and organized that the seated elder, a statue in the round, with fully articulated, asymmetrical body, appears as a "motif," a unit repeated with decorative effect, as in the cloister capitals.

Each figure occupies a little less than the full depth demanded by his position. But since behind each elder we see a common wall and since no two overlap, the represented space appears to be limited to the depth of the elders' seats. The variety of movement

achieved within this narrow space confirms its actuality. Yet the subordination of this movement to a whole composed primarily in line, in which each elder is a unit of a large surface design, provokes our attention before the individual spaces described above.

For how arbitrary are the seating of the elders and the structure of the whole vision! The figures are superposed on narrow ledges so that those below can see only the heels of those above, and the central object is only barely visible to the elders. In the Roman mosaic of the vision in S. Paolo *fuori le mura* the elders are ranged in two rows of which the upper figures are partly concealed by the lower and appear to be behind them. But within the more extended depth of the earlier work there is an even less realistic coordination; for if the figures are turned toward Christ, their heads face the spectator. In Moissac, they are all turned to behold Christ, but they can hardly see him for lack of space to turn in and a plausible viewpoint.

In this respect the tympanum is archaic like the cloister capitals on which the figures are also of relatively high relief, even if less boldly undercut. Whatever overlapping of figures appears in the tympanum is limited to their extremities, so that no one is in lower relief than another. The wings of the lion and bull cover parts of the seraphim's legs, but the bodies of the latter are as salient as the beasts', and no greater depth is effected by the overlapping.

Even the platforms on which the figures are placed are not strictly horizontal planes but sloping surfaces, analogous to the astragals of the cloister. Their pro-

jection is, of course, more considerable, like a narrow stage, but still not enough to permit the full extension of the thighs of a seated figure. The thigh is therefore seen in profile or is placed at an acute angle to the wall. But in the few figures whose legs are extended at right angles to the wall, the thighs are necessarily foreshortened, precisely as in the exceptions on the cloister capitals and as in contemporary drawings. The sculptor has tried to give the legs of Christ their full extension by inclining the lap as if the figure were seated on a sloping surface or were drawing his legs underneath the throne. A similar distortion is practiced on the sloping upper surface of some of the elders' chairs (Figs. 100, 103). We recognize in it the survival of the more archaic vertical planes of the chairs and tables of the cloister.

Though their heads are turned at various angles the figures retain a characteristic axis which reveals the underlying archaism of the whole conception. In only one figure are the shoulders not strictly frontal (Fig. 100). It is true that they cross their legs and extend their arms. But these movements are uniformly restrained and do not modify the simple block of the whole. They suggest in no way the penetration of the background wall, or a complete freedom of gesture. In no figure is the axis of the torso a curved line.

In the one elder whose shoulders are perpendicular to the background, the torso stiffly sustains this position (Fig. 100). The transition from the upper to lower body is therefore unreal. We may observe here how the more sophisticated conceptions of movement, when they appear in an archaic art, are transformed into schematic representations as arbitrary as the most primitive rendering of a figure at rest. The limbs are treated as separate units and combined in disregard of the complex torsion of connecting parts, which makes these movements possible.

That the movements of such figures were conceived as on a flat surface appears from the extension of the instruments and from the distorted positions adopted in order to cross the legs and turn the body in parallel planes (Figs. 108, 109). If they generate no spatial design despite their twisted and restless postures, their limited movements in depth are nevertheless essential to the quality of the tympanum as a whole. The tympanum is so densely filled with irregular solids that hardly a smooth clear surface is visible in the entire work. The endless complication of radial and zigzag lines is paralleled to some extent by the play of projecting limbs. The cross-section of the tympanum at any level is of an extreme complexity and offers analogies to the overlapping and involvement of

shorter lines in plane. How deliberately this circulation of forms within the limited depth of the relief was designed may be seen in the outer garment of the elder in the lower right corner of the tympanum (Fig. 108). It passes behind the right shoulder, under the upper arm, across the forearm and right thigh, and behind the left foot. It is coiled in depth and interlaced with the body like the fantastic beard of the same figure. In the elder above him (Fig. 109) the mantle issues from behind the back through a triangle formed by the flexed arm, as though a knot, and falls behind the right foot which, by a similar design, is twisted around the left leg.

There are several figures in whom the contrast of limbs, though still subordinate to a linear surface design, implies the emergence of a more plastic and spatial relief. It is apparent in the two elders at the left end of the middle row, whose legs are turned toward each other (Fig. 102). In the outer figure the overlapping of the arms, the instrument, and the winding ribbon produces an active recession of forms in space, which is confirmed by the diagonal projection of the right thigh and the inclination of the head and crown. The mantle asserts its spatial character in its inclination from the projecting knee to the right shoulder and in its draping of the left arm.

Yet even in these figures the contrasting limbs are designed primarily on a common surface as directions or lines to which the necessary realization of the individual form of each part gave a more spatial character. The diagonal projection of the legs in both elders was first conceived as a diagonal movement in plane. The shoulders and torso remain parallel to the background and the feet are brought forward to the same plane, though the thighs are at a marked angle to the surface. It is noteworthy that in no instance is a leg bent sharply backward in depth, but in many figures it is inclined diagonally, parallel to the surface (Fig. 111).[101]

The figure of the angel symbolizing Matthew includes the typical distortions resulting from the embodiment of intense movement, designed in a single plane, in figures carved in the round, with an archaic bias toward distinctness, generalized representation, and parallel planes (Fig. 111). His pose suggests a body placed in depth perpendicular or diagonal to the surface of the tympanum; in fact, the prominence of his belly with its rounded contour is clearly that of a figure in profile. Likewise, the outline of his left shoulder, which has been foreshortened, belongs to a profile position. But if we regard the other shoulder we shall see that it does not extend into the wall in the expected direction; it is parallel to the back-

ground like the shoulders of Christ and the seated elders. The whole figure is in consequence distorted; but from this arbitrary twisting results a greater energy of movement. The limbs appear to be all the less constrained. These positions are not really impossible, but they are achieved in actuality only with effort, and are precariously sustained. Such also is the crossing of the angel's legs. The feet are brought to the same plane of the foreground instead of standing one behind the other. We perceive this as the necessary accompaniment of the twisting of the shoulders and the crossing of the arms. The head and hands are opposed above, like the two feet below, as the terminations of the diagonals of a great X which underlies this figure. The extended arm of Christ adds another diagonal to the whole scheme. In accord with this intensity of gesture, the contours of the figure are wavy and zigzag. We have only to follow the outline of the upper part of the figure, the lifted book, the arm, shoulder, and head, and compare it with that of the left side—of the projecting leg, the belly, and the mantle edge—to see that the effect of energy and movement inheres not in the posture alone, but in the play of body and drapery contours as well. The shapes of adjacent objects also contribute to this movement of a single figure. The extended arm of Christ has already been mentioned; observe too the feathers of the wing above the angel's head, the nimbus, and the curved line of the starred mandorla which rises from behind it.

We see from this analysis that the distortion of the body arises more from a linear design than from plastic considerations. To cross the limbs so energetically as to produce an X and a related zigzag silhouette and maintain at the same time the clearer and more characteristic views of the parts of the body required an inconsistency in the natural articulation, which hardly deterred a sculptor to whom the form of the whole body was a pliable expressive aggregate of separate limbs.

The persistence of an archaic system of forms is apparent in the inconsistent directions of the glance and the turn of the head. Because of the universal attraction to Christ we interpret each eye as directed toward him. But in most of the elders, and especially those at the ends, the inclination of the head has only a symbolic and compositional reference to Christ. The eyeballs themselves are perfectly smooth or show an iris or pupil incised at the center of the eye. If the glance were prolonged as a line perpendicular to the horizontal axis of the eyeballs, it would fall in most cases, not on the figure of Christ, but outside the

tympanum, far before him.

This apparent contradiction of the intended glance and the turn of the head is a modern reading foreign to the Romanesque sculptor. The composition was designed as if in one plane and the turn of the head represents a movement on the surface of the tympanum, and not in a depth unformulated and unimagined by the sculptor. The figures appear to us isolated, freely moving three-dimensional objects, but although they are such in substance, they were not entirely such in the conception of the artist. The glance was for him not a direction in three-dimensional space but, like other large movements, an implicit line on the plane surface of the image. A strictly frontal figure like Christ can therefore have no glance; it would presuppose a space outside the image. To determine the intended glance of the Romanesque figures of the tympanum, we should draw lines in the plane of the latter, prolonging the horizontal axis of the eyes. They would then converge approximately to the head of Christ.

If the sculptor admitted the necessary profile views of the heads of the elders directly beneath Christ (Fig. 100), it was not simply because this turn alone was plausible, or more consistent with a spaceless conception than another posture, like that of the shepherds in Byzantine and Gothic art who look up frontally to see the angels. It is motivated also by the dynamic (and, in a sense, kinematic) concentration on Christ achieved by a progressively effected coincidence of the posture and the glance; it conforms to the central position of these heads beneath Christ and their symmetrical pairing below his divergent feet. Since the gaze of a figure is defined by the prolongation of the horizontal axis of the eye, or a line in the plane of the tympanum perpendicular to the vertical axis of the face, a head directly beneath Christ could see him only if turned in a horizontal profile.[102]

In a later sculpture of the same magnitude, the outermost figures would be turned in the sharpest profile and the more central individuals would maintain a three-quarter or frontal position. For since the heads are carved in the round, the spectator from his central viewpoint would see the peripheral profile heads in three-quarters, unless the profile were emphasized. In Moissac, however, each figure is carved as if seen from a point directly opposite and is bound to the whole by a linear and surface, not spatial, design. The insistent representation of twenty-four profiles would have been repugnant to a sculptor devoted to a fuller rendering of parts, and would have, besides, overaccented the subordination to Christ in a

Fig. 115. Church; Detail of Tympanum: Symbol of John

field of which each corner has its varied, distinctive form. Such a profiling would also have produced in each figure a movement in depth and commanded either a profile body, in contradiction of the primarily parallel relief planes of the whole, or a stark uniform contrast of the profile head and frontal body.

The profile heads of several elders in the lowest zone show the considerable elasticity of the style. They indicate that the imaginative sculptor was not rigidly committed to a set archaic method but, as in the capitals of the cloister, could apply more developed forms (perhaps invented in the course of work). This is confirmed by the diversity of eye forms in the elders, which include a range from the most archaic smooth, unincised, inexpressive eyeball to an eye in which the iris is a concavity slightly off both axes of the eyeball. In several elders (Fig. 109) this concavity becomes, because of the inclination of the head, the locus of an active glance, like the more impressionistically modeled eyes of a later art. Only its lack of a consistent spatial relation to the figure of Christ forbids us to identify this conception of the eye with a naturalistic rendering of a glance. Naturalistic details and individuals were sooner created than naturalistic groups.

A marked development in representation is apparent in other parts of the figure beside the eye, and corresponds to the greater complexity of relief and linear design in the tympanum as compared with the cloister capitals. The proportions are still arbitrary, ranging from the superhuman height of Christ and the angels to the dwarfed figures of some of the elders, but they imply a freer choice and a greater knowledge of actual shapes than in the earlier works. For the heads are no longer the preponderant mass that was observed in the cloister; if the elders appear so short, it is partly because of hierarchical distinctions in the proportioning of the various types of figures on the tympanum, partly because of the exigencies of spacing. The larger scale of the whole permitted a greater relief and a more detailed rendering of familiar forms.

The structure of the limbs emerges more clearly from underneath the drapery than in the cloister, though still simplified. The swelling of the calf, the contour of the ankle and foot, are finely observed (Fig. 108) and utilized as important lines of the composition of a figure. The jointing has become looser, so that less distortion results from the movements of hand and foot, and the fingers are bent with greater freedom. No hand in the cloister reveals such precise observation as the left hand of Christ, clasping the book (Fig. 101). On the right wrist are faint traces of a

ridging that correspond to the tendon structure, unobserved in the cloister. Instead of the few conventional positions of the hand admitted in the cloister, the sculptor has produced a great variety, including some distorted hands of unarchaic complexity. The feet likewise show a more refined observation and increased knowledge. Less mobile than the hands, they were sooner copied with an effect of complete accuracy.

The greatest verity was sought in the reproduction of surface ornament, such as the jeweled borders of the garments, the cabochons of the crowns, and the embroidered rosettes of the cushion and cloth behind the figure of Christ. These are of an incredible minuteness and fidelity, in contrast to the broad chiseling of the other surfaces. Such exactitude was already visible in the earlier works of the cloister and it is not surprising in an art which reduces organic forms to regular decorative patterns. In reproducing this ornament the sculptor was engaged not so much in the imitation of nature as in the repetition of a familiar ornamental motif in stone.

The musical instruments are an excellent example of this kind of realistic representation which is simply the reproduction of an object, itself a work of contemporary art. The sculptor fashioned the instrument in stone in its actual dimension and detail, as did the original craftsman in wood. It offered no problem of adjustment to scale or perspective, for it was carved in the round and sometimes even detached from the background. The stone was sufficiently thick to permit a full reproduction without need of foreshortening. The forms were easy to render, since they too were essentially Romanesque creations. From these sculptured artifacts it is possible to reconstruct precisely the instrumentation of the period. Not only have the surfaces been carefully copied, but the strings are noted separately, and in one case a bow has been introduced. Such literalness is nevertheless not unartistic. The position of the instruments, their angles with respect to the seated and variously turned figures, are finely determined. But even the instruments themselves are beautiful and we must concede an aesthetic intention in the precise reproduction of shapes so graceful.

In the modeling of the larger body masses, like the torso and legs, the sculptor reduced the natural variety of surface articulation to a few broad planes. Such is the construction of the figure of Christ, who is divided into several sharply contrasted surfaces, all quite flat, on which numerous folds are inscribed. The richness of surface is primarily linear rather than plastic. Even the rounding of the legs and the hollow of the lap are sacrificed to this impressive architectural severity of the figure. A single broad plane defines the upper legs and lap, another joins the lower legs, in disregard of the concave surface that ordinarily appears between them on so close-fitting a garment.

Of this quadrature of the body structure, the beautiful elder who sits at the extreme left in the middle row is a powerful example (Fig. 99). The thigh and leg have become prismatic blocks; their planes are contrasted like those of the crown of the elder and the sides of his stringed instrument.

The heads of the figures are squared in the manner of archaic Greek sculpture. The contrast of the planes of brow and eyes, of the sides of the nose, of cheeks and jaws, is so sharp that the stereotomic character of the work is brought into striking relief. The head has the appearance of quarried stone and the features seem hewn rather than chiseled. This vigorous construction of the head accents the symmetry of the features. On a wall less sheltered from the sun these heads would invite a more interesting light and shade with abrupt transitions and clearly outlined shadows. The division of planes accords with the conception of drawing, which delineates geometrically correct features, arches the brows high above the eyes, and isolates the parts distinctly to ensure perfect clarity.

Not the head alone but the more complex structure of crown, head, and beard constitutes the sculptured unit. These are united as the separate parts of a building in three dimensions, three superposed storeys, each unlike the other, with clear lines of demarcation. The addition of crown and beard suggests a wonderful variety of plastic combinations. In each head the disposition of hair and crown has a characteristic plan that is uniquely related to the facial structure.

On the crowns, the small cabochons and filigree motifs form an applied surface ornament which rarely modifies the structure or contour of the crown. But the beards are in themselves ornamental patterns, formed by the repetition and symmetrical grouping of locks and curls and the parallel striation of individual hairs, as in the more primitive figures of the cloister piers. But on the tympanum, the sculptor, freer in the use of radial and wavy lines, has produced more varied combinations in the effort to singularize the hair and beard of each of the twenty-four elders. The rich variety of beard and hair seems deliberately cultivated, like the arbitrary breaks and pleatings of the garments and their jeweled borders, rather than a simple imitation of contemporary manners. The elaborateness of the hair recalls classic descriptions of the customs of the Germanic peoples and the earlier Celts.[103] But it is doubtful that the finely combed long hair, beards, and moustaches of the Romanesque tympanum are simply imitations of a historical practice. The braiding of the hair and beard of one elder (Fig. 108) is known earlier in Irish art[104] and in Romanesque sculptures in Toulouse,[105] Saint-Antonin,[106] Verona,[107] Silos,[108] and Chartres,[109] and León.[110]. But these examples are so exceptional that we must regard the form, whether found in life or in art, as an artistic motif, an assimilation of the wavy, mingled strands of hair to a familiar mediaeval ornament. This is especially apparent in the Irish examples which are associated with borders of intricate interlaced bands. Likewise, the spiral locks of the beard of Christ recall the palmette designs of imposts in the cloister. The use of braided and more pronounced radial patterns on the tympanum, as distinguished from the simpler though equally ornamental hair forms of the cloister, corresponds to the heightened linear complexity and movement in the former.

Even though the features have been much more closely observed in the tympanum, the absence of facial expression is almost as marked here as in the cloister. The various combinations of hair do not conceal from us the uniform impersonality of the elders. The emotion of the figures in an apocalyptic experience is hardly indicated by their features. Except for the smile of the Matthew symbol and the left seraph, the heads are altogether impassive. It is remarkable that this peculiar smile should alone among all possible expressions of the face precede the others in both Romanesque and archaic Greek sculpture. The classical archaeologists have sometimes questioned the meaning of this expression and have even doubted that it was designed to represent a smile. But in Moissac it is probably a sign of beatitude or joy before God; in later scenes of the Last Judgment it appears in unmistakable emphasis on the faces of the blessed.[111]

I do not believe that it is simply a religious expression, just as it would be wrong to explain the impassivity of the elders as a consciously constructed image of their dignified attention to Christ or of their changeless nature. The presence of this smile in archaic Greek sculpture and in early arts in China and Central America, which otherwise maintained a common impassivity, calls for another, if only complementary, explanation. The more usual absence of facial expression is readily intelligible in the archaic context of plastically simple forms which are com-

pounded of the stable characteristic aspects of objects. That the smile does occur in Moissac is less strange when we observe its limitation to a few figures and its schematic form. It is a simple curvature of the mouth rather than the revision of the whole face in emotion. Is the smile perhaps the archaic type of all facial expression, the most generalized and contagious form of facial excitement? And is the happiness of the angels in Moissac a theological motif congenial to a sculptor who for the first time was preoccupied with the representation of feeling, just as in later art incidents of extreme suffering are a chosen matter for realistic reproduction? When the wounded soldiers of Aegina grimace with pain, the mouth is turned upward as in the contrary archaic smile.

For the expressive effect of the whole tympanum the introduction of special meanings in the faces of so many little figures would have been a superfluous and distracting effort. We have seen that the common excitement is transmitted in a much more subtle and striking manner by more abstract means. Of these, the elaboration of drapery forms deserves a special description. From the inanimate garments the sculptor derived more numerous and more intricate patterns of movement than from the human figure. In the design of the tympanum the figures are indeed skeletons which without their draperies would possess some articulation but hardly their present intensity.

The complication of drapery forms was inevitable in an expressive linear style which had for its chief subject matter the clothed human figure, and which was associated with an ornament of traditional linear complexity. In an art that rarely represented facial expressions, limited gesture to a few conventional movements, and conceived nude forms only in rare religious contexts, the greatest possibilities of expression, of surface enrichment, and of linear design lay 'in the garment. The most complex drapery forms, the most freely meandering movement of folds, are significantly found in those schools of Romanesque art which also display their dynamic goal in the extraordinary elongation of the figures and their unstable postures. But in Auvergne and Tuscany, where the garments cling more closely to the figure and are less intricate, the figures appear squat and lethargic.

The rendering of a fluent, mobile element like drapery hardly seems upon first thought a likely task of an art as archaic as the sculpture of Moissac. But the process which simplifies the nude body and selects clear positions and regular monumental groupings also orders the succession of folds in parallel or concentric surfaces. If these retain, in spite of the

archaic treatment, the mobile quality of actual garments and, in fact, an even more extreme activity, it is because the processes of representation are in this style subordinate to an essentially dynamic expressive end. In the following analysis, we shall see that the drapery forms of the tympanum are unplastic linear abstractions of a geometric character, and that the great freedom and energy of movement spring from the arbitrary combination of simple stereotypes, in many ways unlike the forms of actual folds.

In the drapery of a Gothic or more recent sculpture, single folds are inseparable from the whole; they are more plastic than the Romanesque and mingle in such a way that whatever their patterning and linear organization they are perceived at once as parts of a common structure. We can trace no groove without observing the influence of neighboring forms on its expansion and movement; its origin is usually indefinite or vague. On the early Romanesque figures, folds may be more readily isolated, despite their apparent complexity. The entire pleating of the lower edges constitutes a system independent of the upper portion, while the single grooves on the torso and legs are separate, unplastic elements attached to the garment like the buttons or fringes on a modern dress. The drapery resembles in this respect the forms of the figure itself. Just as eyes, nose, and lips are separate elements compounded to form the whole, so the folds are distinguishable entities on the costume, no matter how involved and contrasted.[112] This point, which seems obvious, is worth making since it confirms the pervasive character of the processes of representation and the style, whether occupied with animate or inanimate things.

The costume of the tympanum figures consists of the following pieces: a long, undecorated undergarment that falls to the ankles, a tunic reaching to a point just below the knees, usually bordered at the collar and lower edge with jewelry, and a simple mantle, only rarely buckled. Not one figure wears shoes. All but the two seraphim and the symbols are crowned. The crowns are not of one form, but round, square, polygonal, and are adorned with a variety of lozenge and simple foliate patterns. The elders are variously clothed; some wear all three garments, others only two, and on several we can detect but one robe. The ornaments also vary, both in their distribution on the collars and other borders and in the motifs employed. The system of design is uniform and traditional. It consists of the repetition, in alignment, of one motif or of two in alternation. The lozenge and the rosette are most common, while the simple bead or pearl is the usual filling of the inter-spaces. The high relief of some lozenges, the circum-scribed circles, the carving of facets on both lozenge and circular units, point to the imitation of actual cabochons. Filigree appears in the beaded borders of some rosettes and in the beads attached to long, fine filaments.

The variety of costume is especially interesting since it is not commanded by distinctions of rank. It is an arbitrary choice which reflects at the same time a realistic predilection for diversity and a style that multiplies oppositions. It is in turn a source of textural variations and formal contrasts.

In the figures of the tympanum we are hardly aware of distinct robes, but of numberless pleats, folds, bor-ders, broken edges, and overlapping planes of cloth, at first difficult to disengage. There are no clearly exposed, undivided surfaces on the garments. But this seeming chaos of drapery includes only a few types of pleats and breaks. These are arbitrary schematizations of actual folds multiplied, without exact reference to an existing model, for enrichment of sculptural sur-face and line.

On the tympanum the bare incised line common in the most primitive arts is exceptional and subordi-nate. It appears on the sleeves of some of the elders as a decorated border or as a means of rendering a par-ticular texture, sometimes as a faint wrinkle at the elbow joint. Its ornamental function is apparent also in the figures of Christ and the Matthew symbol as a line accompanying a more plastic or salient parallel fold.

Instead, the doubled line already described in the reliefs and capitals of the cloister is more commonly used. It is limited, however, to the figure of Christ, the seraphim, and the symbol of Matthew. Sometimes it is repeated in simple concentric loops or radial curves, as on the arms of the seraphim; sometimes two sets of such lines, proceeding from opposite sides of a limb or garment, interlock in alternation. This device was familiar in later classic art; it arose from the stylization of the great, deep-grooved folds of a suspended classical garment. It occurs, for example, on the Victories of the podium of the Arch of Con-stantine and on numerous figures in the province of Gaul.[113] But in Moissac, the classic subordination of these lines has been carried still further; they are only superficial markings of the surface of the figures; their repetition forms a secondary ornament beside the more powerful lines of the legs and torso.

The figures are swathed in their tunics as if ban-daged by rolls of heavy cloth. The torsos are divided by concentric or parallel lines formed by the contours of these superposed bands. A similar banding covers the arms and legs, but here the lines are often radial. The garment is of so thick a cloth that the outline of a limb is stopped or broken by the succession of over-lapping bands. On the central figures of the tym-panum a finely incised line accompanies such folds. On the thigh of the Matthew symbol this incision is doubled. The alternate interlocking of two systems of adjacent concentric folds, such as occurs in the dou-ble folds, is also applied to these prominent lines between the legs of the right seraph.

The forms described so far determine for the most part curved lines and concentric groups. They are the forms of draperies fixed to the body and inscribed on its surface, and hence limited to simple lines, whether curved or straight. They are not among the more effective devices of movement employed on the tympanum, but their restless character is evident in two peculiarities of their application. They are de-signed perpendicular to the axis of the limb which they cover, and hence in contrast to its larger form. We shall grasp this effect more readily if we imagine a column banded with horizontal rings instead of flut-ings parallel to its axis. Imagine the corresponding Greek figures with the folds of their garments, not falling in easy verticals, but grooved horizontally about their bodies. In the second place, by the over-lapping of such bands of cloth in concentric shells, the large simplified expanse of the leg or torso be-comes broken and incomplete, like a telescoped ob-ject. The surface loses its definiteness and, though barely modeled, is perceived as a composite of numer-ous minor surfaces. An animated plastic effect is achieved here with a minimum of relief. The device remains archaic in the similarity of these bands and in their regular succession.

These folds are too subordinate to the human figure to have suggested possibilities of more intense linear interplay to a sculptor little concerned with anatom-ical detail and plastic variety. But wherever the gar-ment is only partly attached to the figure and at least one of its ends hangs freely, the design acquires a remarkable richness from the elaboration of the con-sequent broken contour. Yet the independence of an-atomical constraint does not imply an unrestrained fancy. On the contrary, the units of a hanging bit of drapery are singularly conventional and limited to as few basic forms as the ornament of prehistoric pottery. But these elements occur in such a variety of com-binations that the poverty of motif is hardly apparent.

Suspended drapery never falls here as one broad

mass. It is subdivided by numerous parallel or radial pleats, all equally flat. The pleats are pressed so close to each other that no arris confronts the spectator. But in contradiction of this piling up of flat, almost parallel layers, their lower contours form larger angles than their superimposed surfaces, as if the edge of the garment were diagonal rather than horizontal.

This is an archaic device, analogous to the vertical surfaces of the tables and seats represented on the cloister capitals and the peculiar polygonal ends of the garments of the apostles. The lower edges are clearly exposed as if they were parts of a system of pleats forming angles of forty-five degrees. We have seen this same convention in the cloister—sometimes, as in the east gallery, it was even more arbitrarily applied. It is also familiar in the early sculptures of Greece and China.[114]

In this contour the artist reveals the full expansion of folds, of which the main surface is partly concealed, and makes the overlapping of drapery perfectly clear. The edge is defined by ascending and descending, less frequently horizontal, sequences of meandering and zigzag lines. The rhythmic movement of well-distributed, alternately advancing and receding lines, unequally accented by relief and shadow, is heightened by the play of the verticals they terminate. The simplest zigzag is of perfectly straight lines, all diagonal. The angle ranges from ninety degrees to very acute openings.

Often the pleating is more dense and intricate; the tucked surface is brought far under the outer layer, and meander patterns of extremely narrow interval are produced by the lower edges. Not content with the simple regularity of the common zigzag, the sculptor breaks each of its lines in two, forming an inner obtuse angle, as if the pleats were folded in the middle. Although the pleat remains as flat as before, its broken lower contour suggests an equally broken surface. But it is primarily an enrichment of line that is sought in this device, although the more complex form might well have been suggested by real garments.

Beside these fan-shaped pleatings, a symmetrical form analogous to the peculiar polygonal patterning of the lower edge of the costume in the cloister is often employed on the tympanum. It may be defined as a symmetrical system of pleats of which the lower contours ascend diagonally to the central fold. The folds between Christ's legs are a clear example of this form. The border of his outer tunic has been disposed to produce two such groups of zigzags.

In several elders such contours are independent of lengthy pleats but terminate a small bell-like structure at the ankle, attached to the main body of the garment by a thin pleat or even a knot.

At Christ's left ankle such a fold is monstrously expanded without a clear motivation by the form of the garment or the movement of the figure. The long wavy fold that attaches the fanlike pleats to the tunic is difficult to explain as a feature of an actual costume. This stem appears to be a ribbon or loose end of clothing projecting from an invisible undergarment. It is based on a more intelligible model, of which the parts have been combined without reference to their original relation. In classic and Carolingian art, on garments rendered as if blown by the wind, a long diagonal fold terminated in a domical structure that flew behind.[115] The diagonal was the index of the swiftness of the movement; the smaller its angle with the ground the greater the velocity and the current which produced the fold at its end. The figure of Christ bearing a long cross in the canon-tables of the Gospels of Saint-Médard-de-Soissons is a clear illustration of the original type.[116] In Moissac the connection of the terminal structure with the central part of the tunic has been misunderstood. It is attached to the end of the garment, yet the copied diagonal fold is added to connect the blown portion with the unmoved central part to which neither belongs.

There is another inconsistent but effective detail in the drapery of Christ which is a traditional survival of an ancient, misunderstood form. A hanging fold across the torso, passing under the drapery of the right arm, is a remnant of the sash formed in late classic art by the disposition of the mantle across the waist and abdomen. In classic figures the folds that covered the right arm emerged from under this sash as on the tympanum. The Christ of the mosaic of Santa Pudenziana in Rome is an example of the prototype of the Romanesque figure.[117] Here the mantle thrown across the body is no slight suspended band but a broad sash that covers the undertunic. As in Moissac the earlier Christ of the mosaic is enthroned and extends his right hand in a similar benediction. Although the original function of this bit of drapery has been lost in the sculpture, the artist has distinguished it clearly from the adjoining folds. He has accented its continuity with the extended arm in the interception of the opposed concentric, convex lines of the torso; and hence its anaxial or eccentric correspondence to the symmetrical curves of the lion and the bull. By these oppositions the axial figure of Christ in the center of the encircling group becomes even more unstable, more active.

The simplicity of the linear devices described above

has its counterpart in the modeling or relief of the garments. The obvious definiteness of the single contours, which is called by a just metaphor, "geometrical," is matched by the relative regularity of the larger surfaces. The garment envelops the body closely without plastic self-assertion. The multiplied pleats do not alter the surface of the limbs but determine a slightly thicker shell at certain points. If the drapery modifies the underlying body structure at all, it is by a simplification which shapes one broad plane across the legs to cover the hollow ordinarily between them. On this plane the folds are superposed, each quite flat, or incised. Where the folds hang or fall outside the figure they are attached to a chair or background wall or form a surface parallel to the latter. Even in those pleats which are slightly diagonal to the wall, as at the left ankle of Christ, the separate surfaces are flat, and there is little or no contrast with curved forms, and no irregular flow. The profiles or sections of folds illustrate the archaic character of the relief. The development of relief is measured not by the absolute depth of cutting but by the depth represented and by the variety of section of boss and hollow. In the tympanum the relief is less the result of varied modeling or shaping of surfaces than of the superposition of similar enveloping layers on a projecting mass. The extension of limbs carries with it the salience of the garment and its suspended folds; but these are themselves unarticulated and show no tensions or movement in a third dimension independent of the structure beneath them. The effect is of great massy surfaces with intricately cut boundaries and a network of lines.

A departure from the vigorous application of this conception appears in the shallow fluting of some vertical folds, and in the corrugation of broad surfaces, like the torso, by grooves zigzag in section. But the stylized form of these departures shows how well established is the linear rather than plastic conception of drapery. Even in the few folds of curved rather than zigzag or meander contour, the surfaces retain the simplicity of the others. The relief of the garments is essentially no different from that of a pressed pleated ribbon. This is the more evident in the figures seated near the frame adjoining the fine meander border.

Hence the draperies invite little contrast of light and shade except along contours. We are reminded of the plastic character of the undraped primitive figure. The contours of drapery at Moissac are often undercut, lifted above the background, but the raised surfaces are barely articulated in a third dimension. The drapery design, so far as modeling is concerned, is

therefore in no opposition to the principles governing the high relief and vigorous salience of the bodies. When it covers them, the drapery is a simple shell, richly adorned by concentric or radial lines, and where it leaves the bodies it forms in turn a flat mass in a low relief.

The multiplying of layered surfaces, however unplastic, remains a striking feature of the relief of the tympanum. It suggests the unsuccessful effort to achieve a varied plastic form by the addition of unplastic elements, like theoretical unextended points arrayed to form a line. But this is not really the function of such an accumulation of layers of relief. Its evident effect has already been observed in the description of the ringlike folds of the legs and torso, which produce a busy contrast of lines and an activation of the larger surface. By the overlapping of pleats a similar, if not more broken, restless surface is produced despite the flatness of the whole. The larger planes seem to be covered by irregular shreds, like the surface of an object intricately wrapped innumerable times.

The ornamented borders of the garments are important parts of the drapery design. They provide a surface roughened, pitted, minutely grooved and bossed, in contrast to the smoother parts of the gar-

Fig. 118. Church; Detail of Tympanum: Elder of Bottom Row

ment. Originally these jeweled bands were painted, like the rest of the tympanum, and this contrast of textures must have been reinforced by color. How the drapery design was affected by the polychromy we can no longer say, for no large tympanum has preserved its original color intact. At Conques, where the fading color is still visible, the tones are so blond and light, so delicate, that they are little more than a vague ornament; perhaps no plastic accentuation was intended, and no strong pattern results. I think it is not improbable that on the tympanum of Moissac the crowns and all other metallic details were gilded; that the undergarments and mantles were distinguished by sharply contrasting tones; that the background itself was painted and entered more prominently into the design.

The prominence of the jeweled detail indicates the primitive character of the art, not because a barbaric taste for richness is reflected, but because the effect of a colorful or rich relief is demanded from applied surface ornament more than from plastic variation. In the later art it is by furrowing deeply and chiseling the body and the garments to yield an endless play of boss and hollow that a diversified surface is obtained. The use of jeweled detail in broad flat bands is in a sense antiplastic. This is apparent in Byzantine painting in figures of monarchs and angels who are laden with richly ornamented garments. The modeling of the limbs and folds, which is common in other figures, even in the same works, is less pronounced.

It is clear from this survey of the details of drapery on the tympanum that although they include all the elements of drapery form present in the cloister they are closest as a group to the capitals of the south gallery. In the latter were observed the same proliferation of folds, the swathing of the body in numerous pleats, and the jeweled detail. The edges of garments are often broken into meandering lines like those of the tympanum. Like the latter, they are predominantly angular and sometimes extend beyond the outlines of the body as if blown by the wind. In the elders, the incised double fold is rarely employed although it appears on the garments of the taller figures of the tympanum. The chief differences between the drapery style of the portal and that of the south gallery are in the relation of the unit or small detail to the whole figure and in the richness of effect. On the tympanum the cutting of the folds is more vigorous and powerful; the contours are more vivacious and irregular, and the whole surface is more diversified by the pleating than on the capitals. The banding of the torso is never as prominent on the latter as on the tympanum. The extension of this concentric banding to the legs does not occur in the cloister.

* * * * *

A few words, finally, on the animals which are carved no less beautifully than the human figures. Taken down from the tympanum, and viewed separately (Figs. 113, 114, 115), these three beasts would be regarded as supreme masterpieces of animal representation, comparable to certain archaic Greek and Chinese sculptures. The lion and the bull are a single conception. For such a combination of elasticity and power in animal bodies we must turn to the monstrous lions discovered in Southern China by the Ségalen Mission.[118] So intense is their concentration on the figure of Christ that the twist of the head seems to motivate the entire body; the legs are reduced to puny projections.

The sculpturing of the bodies shows the same contrast of broad chiseling and closely observed detail as the human figures. It is especially clear in the heads which are rendered in a powerful and original manner, unlike any familiar beasts. The lion's head was an especial delight to the artist, who lavished on it an obsessive attention in his effort to make the imagined beast more credible by the amount of recognizable detail. The eye has been carved with greater care than that of any human figure; the iris has been incised, the corners of the eye deepened, and the lids clearly demarcated. In a like manner, the muzzle and brows have been painstakingly detailed. I have already mentioned the grand movements of the tails and wings of the animals. The eagle alone is inactive, but the contrasted directions of his head and body create an effect of tension, increased by the tight clutching of his scroll which is wound spirally. The carving of the imbricated feathers is of a subtle perfection in its variation of the same unit by the simplest means.

The position of the eagle (Fig. 115) involves an extreme twisting of his head, for both head and body are in profile but turned in opposite directions. This fact is not admitted by the sculptor, who has represented the difficult movement without indication of strain or distortion. Is the contrast of the eagle's head and body an intended parallel to the corresponding man-symbol of Matthew, who is subject to a similar torsion? Their contours have a related upper and lower projection toward Christ and a similar intervening hollow. But even the lion has been shaped into an analogous construction: the head is violently turned, contrary to the movement of the body, while a large wing rises from his neck, extended like the arms and book of the Matthew symbol.

THE LINTEL

The tympanum rests on a great lintel with a decoration no less radiant than the figures above (Fig. 119). It is 5.68 meters long and .76 wide, and is composed of three horizontal slabs of Pyrenees marble, reinforced in the rear by other slabs to sustain the huge mass of the tympanum. On its outer surface is carved a frieze of ten rosettes encircled by a cable which issues from the jaws of curly-snouted monsters at the two ends (Fig. 99).[119] The three blocks are not of identical size or shape and are so cut that the symmetrical inner jointings are stepped to ensure a more secure fitting and a better distribution of the weight.[120]

The unit rosette motif consists of eight leaves of acanthus form radiating from a central circular knob or petaled flower. Except in two instances, the leaves are symmetrically disposed with respect to the axes of the slab. The leaf is not the familiar soft or spiky classic form, but a peculiar stylized version that approaches in some details the conventionalized palmette. A radial five-lobed structure, with curled or arched lower lobes, rises from a symmetrical two-lobed stalk as from a vase. On each side the two inferior lobes of the leaf are tangent to those of the neighboring leaves and, together with them, enclose two eyelets as in the classic Corinthian capital—the inner, tall, ovoid, and deep-cut; the outer, broad, crescent, and shallow. Each lobe is bisected by a ridge or vein issuing radially from the central axial ridge of the whole leaf. The lobes are otherwise smooth and regular and, with the exception of the curled ones, symmetrical and tonguelike in shape.

In the triangular surfaces between the large rosettes are also carved acanthus leaves. But these are stylized to resemble trilobed half-palmettes or the profile acanthus of late Roman rinceaux. They are grouped, four in a triangle, and issue from an acanthus wrapping at its base, like a great plant with four waving leaves. Two leaves diverge horizontally, the others vertically, in a symmetrical pattern.

At the tangent point of two rosettes the encircling cable passes through a narrow sheath. But the sixth, seventh, and eighth rosettes (counting from left to right) are not tangent. They are separated by mascarons—chinless monsters like the Chinese Tao-Tieh—through whose heads the cable moves. Between the sixth and seventh the interspace is large enough to permit the insertion of a heavy fruit-and-blossom motif common in Quercy and Limousin.[121]

The effect of this beautiful frieze is one of intense and sustained movement because of the recurrent radiation. Not only the main rosette motif but the subordinate fillings of the interspaces are composed radially. The simple alignment of the rosettes in horizontal order contrasts with the richness of small centrifugal details. Even these, when observed closely, form the elements of simpler circular schemes. For the design is not only of the repeated rosettes and their prominent central knobs; the hollows between

Fig. 119. Church; Detail of Lintel: Undersurface of Lintel

the lobes produce flowerlike patterns. Thus each rosette is a system of concentric circular motifs issuing in widening ripples from the petaled knob. The diffusion of the larger structure in small details gives the whole a liveliness and sculptural richness akin to the tympanum above. And as in the figure sculpture, the apparent regularity of the whole is modified in places by delicate departures from the expected spacing and forms. The even number of rosettes, the variety of knob structure, petaled in five rosettes and simply ridged concentrically in three, the inequalities of interspacing, the anaxial position of two rosettes,[122] the unequal projection of the monsters at the ends, the spiral grooving of the cable of the three left rosettes and the smooth surface on the others—all these are not accidents of hand labor, but designed, since the variations of the left side are balanced by contrasts on the right, while the common details are too finely executed to permit a judgment of negligence or incompleteness.

More remarkable than the linear design and division of the lintel is the character of its relief. Each rosette is a concave surface, like a shallow circular dish set within a wall. The leaves are curved in depth, and the central knob is flush with the flat outer surface of the frieze. Examined more closely, the rosette is not the dish, but its decoration in extremely low relief. Such a style of carving is unique. It cannot be compared directly with the imitation of a wall encrusted with faience dishes, like the facade of the town hall of Saint-Antonin, near Moissac. Such a wall is itself uncarved, while in Moissac the interspaces are also ornamented, and the central knob is flush with them. The outer plane of the lintel is subordinate to the concave themes. In ordinary relief the chief motif is salient from the uniform background plane or is contrasted with the dark shapes of deeply cut interspaces. Sometimes two (or more) patterns of unequal salience constitute the ornament on a common background, but both are flat or parallel in plane. In Moissac the distinction between foreground and background is abolished by the concave modeling of the frieze. We seem to look into the negative mold of a more salient band. By these concavities is achieved a plastic effect with the least assertion of relief. Compare this method with the relief of the tympanum on which the figures, almost detached from the wall, have only a superficially modeled surface. They are alike in the contrast of the relief of the larger units with the subordinate flat details. But the lintel is foreign to the style of the tympanum. Even as a mold of a more obvious convex form, the lintel is not analogous to the reliefs above or to the ornament that frames the tympanum. The dense expanded foliate forms in the lowest possible relief, as well as the repeated concavity, itself shallow, seem to be inconsistent with the massive projection of the figures. The thick vegetation of the archivolt is a more evident decorative analogue of the tympanum relief.

The lintel is an un-Romanesque element in the portal, yet is apparently in place and participates in the design of the whole. It might even be said that its un-Romanesque features are essential to its accord with the whole, and that its discrepant relief is a contribution to an energetically contrasted animated scheme. A more positive and direct congruence in the radial design has already been observed; the concavities serve the same end in promoting a movement between the central knob and the circumference of each rosette.

A lintel of flat rosettes would be insignificant beneath the tympanum; not only would a plastic accent be lacking, but the radial design of the leaves would be lost in the dense all-over patterning of the band. A lintel of convex giant rosettes would be plastically intrusive beneath the row of seated elders and disturb the iconographic hierarchy of the portal. The radial leaves would be less effectively centrifugal, as in an inverted flower. Granted the pattern of rosettes, the existing relief seems most proper to the forms of the tympanum. It is, in fact, anticipated on the latter in the great diversity of rosette ornaments embroidered on the garments of the figures.

When we examine the undersurface of the lintel (Fig. 119) we understand more readily the un-Romanesque character of the main design. For this lower surface, which has been frequently cited but never reproduced, is carved with an earlier ornament and betrays in its style a hand of the seventh century A.D. It consists of a narrow band of acanthus and vine rinceaux, bordered by geometric spiral scrolls, the whole so low in relief and of such delicate execution that its details are barely visible. The vine pattern occupies the two eastern blocks, the acanthus, the western. Anglès was mistaken in writing that the three blocks did not always belong together because of the difference in the ornament of the lower surface.[123] For the three bands are of identical breadth and their borders agree perfectly. If on one band the vine replaces the acanthus, their styles are identical. It is only the abrupt transition from one to the other that justifies the inference that although originally parts of one frieze, they have been reemployed with the omission of an intermediate strip.

The lintel consists of reemployed ancient blocks of which the original style of ornament has been maintained not only in the decorated surfaces preserved, but in those more recently carved. A similar block in the museum of Cahors, undoubtedly of the early Christian-Merovingian period, also includes such rosettes; they are derived, like those of Moissac, from ancient Roman types.[124] The retrospective copying of ancient art might have been inferred without knowledge of the models from the character of the ornament itself, which in relief and motif is un-Romanesque and distinct from the surrounding capitals and moldings.

The lintel has a more general interest for the interpretation of historic arts. It is often supposed that the unity of a work—and the tympanum and lintel are a single work—requires the formal analogy of its parts, and that only those foreign elements are incorporated in a style which are exactly congruent with the rest. But the lintel, which is obviously in harmony with the tympanum, displays quite different principles of relief. There is no question that the art of the seventh century is in style distinct from the Romanesque, yet in this work the close imitation of the earlier style, reproduced with a precision that has misled scholars to suppose the whole work an ancient piece,[125] is compatible with the surrounding Romanesque forms. We learn from this example that the analogy of elements in a work of art is not necessarily pervasive or complete, and that stylistically unlike forms may coexist within a coherent whole. The relations between forms are more crucial and determinative than the form elements themselves. Hence the possible absorption of features from the most remote arts in the Romanesque, without the effect of an eclectic or unintegrated style. The judgment of unintegration is of imperfectly coordinated, not of anomalous, elements.

I must mention, however—if merely to exclude the argument that the lintel is in its entire decoration a reemployed work—the distinctly Romanesque details in its carving. If the carving were ancient, its coherence with the Romanesque tympanum would be even more surprising, and would lead us to suspect an enormous extrapolation in the theory that unity or the quality of work inheres in all its details because of the absolutely integrated thought or perception of its maker. We have only to place the two corner beasts beside the lower symbolic animals of the vision to see that they are decidedly Romanesque in type, although flattened to accord with the subtle relief of the lintel. The disproportionately small legs, and the flat thighs pressed close to the body, recur in them; while the

deeply sunken eyes and prominent frontal ridges are precisely as in the lion of St. Mark. But there is even better evidence that the same hand carved tympanum and lintel. The monstrous head in the lower left corner of the tympanum, from whose jaws issues the meander ribbon, is an almost exact replica, in both shape and function, of the head of the left monster of the lintel. Both have the peculiar curled snouts that suggest the elephant. Nor can it be said in possible reply that the tympanum master copied the already existent lintel in carving such details, for they are unknown in this form in earlier art, though ultimately based on ancient traditions. There are still other indications of the unity of the two works. The two mascaron heads serving as interspaces reproduce exactly the head on the lower right of the tympanum (Fig. 108). They reappear also in the narthex on a console block and are carved on the intricately ornamented outer jambs of the south porch. The fruit and blossoms issuing from the jaws of the left mascaron of the lintel have their exact parallels in sculptures at Beaulieu, Souillac, Cahors, and Martel, all products of the school which produced the portal of Moissac.

There are also elementary considerations of design that refute the argument. The ornament of the ends is perfectly adapted to its position. The repeated rosettes and knobs are like the elders aligned on the zone above, while the density of the carved ornament, filling the surface completely, and its circular, radial design recall the central group of the tympanum. The lintel is conceived in such harmony with the tympanum that they must have been planned as parts of one scheme of decoration.

THE RELIEFS OF THE PORCH

As on the cloister capitals we observed the style of the pier reliefs in a narrative context, so the corresponding manner of the later sculptors of Moissac is visible in the reliefs of the inner walls of the porch (Figs. 120, 121).

Their style has long been recognized as more recent than that of the tympanum, but the differences are such that the two works cannot be far apart in date. The sculptures of the jambs and trumeau which sustain the tympanum belong to the same period as the porch.

On the east wall are scenes from the Infancy of Christ; on the west, the parable of Lazarus and Dives and the punishment of Avarice and Female Unchastity. Little capitals with figures, tormented in the flames by demons or attacked by monsters, paraphrase the Last Judgment. On the east jamb which supports

Fig. 120. Church; Sculptures on East Inner Wall of Porch

Fig. 121. Church; Sculptures on West Inner Wall of Porch

the lintel is carved Isaiah with a scroll prophesying the virgin birth. On the corresponding west jamb, near the reliefs of the parable and the punishments, is Peter, the patron of the abbey, with the keys of heaven. The intermediate trumeau is sculptured with two unnimbed figures of uncertain name. The western figure is bald and has a wrinkled brow like Paul in the cloister and in reliefs at Silos and Arles. The other bears a scroll instead of a book and is probably a prophet, corresponding to Isaiah, like the similar figures in Lombard churches.

The abbot, Roger (1115–1131), is represented on the exterior south wall of the porch, high up on an engaged column (Fig. 146). Another figure, in monastic dress—possibly St. Benedict—stands on a similar column on the other side of the arch (Fig. 145). On the crenellations above the porch are enwalled two figures blowing horns, like watchmen of the fortified church (Fig. 157). The cornice beneath them, crowning the porch, is carried by sculptured modillions of which several are modern restorations.

The reliefs of the porch are not arranged in simple alignment or superposition, but a special architecture, independent of the structure of the wall, is applied to it to frame the reliefs (Figs. 120, 121). They agree in this respect with the sculptures of Poitou, Angoumois, and Saintonge, which are similarly set under arcatures applied to the surface of the wall. But they differ from them in the extension of one scene (the Magi) under two arches, and the superposition of two under a single arch. The independence of architecture and sculpture was already seen in the tympanum, which is composed of separate blocks applied to the wall, and offers no strict correspondence of figures and blocks as in Gothic portals.[126] The designer of the porch not only disregards the character of the wall in the applied members, but even the latter in the distribution of the sculptures among them.[127] This is hardly the unity of structure and decoration which a doctrinaire aesthetic theory has judged to be the essential character of mediaeval architecture, in contrast to Renaissance and Baroque styles. Actually, the grouping of architectural elements on these walls is nearer to the Baroque in principle, and we might number the Romanesque among the early styles in which investigation detects analogies to Baroque art.

The columns framing the superposed reliefs have the character of a giant order enclosing two rows of minor arches and colonnettes. In Romanesque churches, like Saint-Sernin in Toulouse, the bays of the nave have a related elevation, with great shafts rising to the base molding of the barrel vault and enclosing two superposed arches. But in Moissac the columns themselves carry a dominant arch, and the vault springs from a tall frieze placed above it like an attic storey.

The paneling of the inner walls of the porch is designed in a free, asymmetrical manner. The arched fields are framed on one side (south) by vertical bands of richly carved ornament; on the other, by the slender colonnettes of the portal which are noticeably taller than the carved bands; and above, by large friezes sculptured with narrative scenes. There is no podium below. Not only is the frame of the arched fields varied on all four sides, but the internal divisions of the fields are not maintained or acknowledged in the bounding areas by either moldings or ornament. The surface of the inner walls of the porch appears therefore crowded and irregular; the axis of the symmetrical sculptured panels does not coincide with the central axis of the entire wall; and no common background is visible behind this accumulation of sculptures, friezes, and frames.

The arbitrariness of the architecture may be illustrated by the following details. The arches are bordered by a semicircular molding strip, intercepted at the sides by the outer jambs of the portal and the vertical friezes that terminate the walls of the porch. A cornice surmounts the arches, although a horizontal frieze is placed above it. It rests on the busts of caryatids with uplifted hands, while in the spandrels of the arches are carved salient heads in imitation of water spouts or modillions, here functionless. To lend some architectural character to the subdivision of the arcatures into upper and lower panels, trefoils resting on slender, barely visible colonnettes are inscribed within the semicircular arches.

The moldings are not continuous with those of the tympanum. The barrel vault of the porch springs from the torus above the upper horizontal friezes, at a level higher than the capitals of the tympanum archivolt, while the cornice beneath the friezes is higher than the crown moldings of the trumeau and the supporting walls of the portal. Except for the base moldings common to the portal and the walls of the porch, the horizontal lines of the two are discontinuous. At Beaulieu the horizontals of porch and portal coincide; but the porch of Cahors is in this respect disposed more like that of Moissac. Although the porch and tympanum of Moissac are not contemporary, it is doubtful that the discontinuity proceeds from the difference of time alone or even serves to indicate the fact. The alternation of horizontals is too well sustained to be accidental.

The asymmetry of the architecture of the side walls, in shifting the axis toward the portal, subordinates their sculptures to the tympanum and relates them more closely to the figures of the jambs. Had the column stood in the axis of the wall, it would have imposed a corresponding center on the crowning frieze, which is by its very nature, with its horizontal sequence of narrative themes, an unsymmetrical member. It would have given the inner walls of the porch an isolated, self-sufficient, centralized character inconsistent with the religious and plastic priority of the tympanum.

The salient cornice diminishes the apparent height of the sculptured surface and thereby subordinates it again to the tympanum which, by the same device, produces an impression of still greater height. The isolation of a frieze above the reliefs of the side walls corresponds to the clear horizontal bands of the elders and the rosettes, and its contrast with the vertical panels below maintains the contrast of the elders and lintel with the trumeau and jambs of the portal.

The superposed friezes also offer to our perception of static forces a more solid support than a pair of arches on tall slender colonnettes. By a similar calculation the arches are of rectangular section and unmolded, in active contrast to the richness of surface carving everywhere apparent. If the architectural framework of the reliefs is a free composition imposed on the wall, its design is well adapted to the sculptural whole of the porch and portal and is consistent in character.

The sculptures of each side of the porch do not unite to form one great relief like the tympanum; nor are the main contours distinct enough to determine a single scheme dominating the whole. But we shall see presently that an effort was made to surmount the barriers of separate subject matter and architectural frames by a common movement and related forms.

The reliefs diminish in height in ascending order. At the same time they broaden, so that the middle panels, which are united into a single large field either by the subject (Adoration of the Magi) or the common design (the Death of Dives and his Punishment), mediate between the tall vertical panels below and the single horizontal friezes above. The arches within the scenes of the Presentation, the idols of Heliopolis, and the banquet of Dives unite the horizontal friezes more intimately with the arcaded reliefs below.

The reliefs, moreover, are not on the same plane. The lowest figures (Annunciation, Visitation, Lux-

uria) stand under trefoiled arches which form the edges of a sloping roof structure. On the eastern reliefs this roof is realistically rendered with carved slate or tile imbrications.[128]

The panels above are set more deeply under the large arches and the flat, molded trefoils. We can more readily appreciate this recession in observing the relation of the roof above the figure of Unchastity to the ground plane of the scene of Dives' death above it.

With this diminution in the height of the ascending reliefs their figures change in proportions. The most elongated and slender are in the lower panels, the squattest, in the upper horizontal scenes.[129] On

Fig. 122. Church; Detail of East Wall of Porch: Adoration of the Magi—the Magi

the east wall this gradation of scale corresponds to the narrative order of incidents. For the lowest scenes are the earliest (Annunciation and Visitation) and those of the upper frieze the last of the cycle (Flight into Egypt). On the west wall, however, the story of Lazarus and Dives begins on the frieze above and terminates below in the central panels. On the lowest band are represented the Punishment of Avarice and Unchastity.

Whether this contrast in the order of incidents is a stylistic correlate of an asymmetrical architecture and restless animated figures or the consequence of an iconographic program is difficult to decide.[130] The episodic parable of Lazarus and Dives could hardly be fitted into the two lowest panels which were reserved for twin pairs of opposed elongated figures. There are other contrasts and irregularities in the sequence of action that suggest an aimlessness of composition surprising in Romanesque art. But analysis will reveal an underlying order and purpose.

In the horizontal frieze of the east wall the episodes of the Presentation in the Temple and the Flight into Egypt seem to form a continuous narrative (Figs. 120, 4, 5, 124, 125). But these scenes do not move in a single direction; if we attempted, without knowledge of the texts represented, to determine the order of events and the relation of certain figures to each other we would be very much puzzled. The Presentation, the first in order of time, moves from left to right; but the Flight moves in the opposite direction. At the extreme left of the panel is the city of Heliopolis with its falling idols. The successive incidents diverge from a common center; and with a perfect adroitness in dramatic arrangement the artist has placed between the two scenes a figure common to them and pointing in both directions. This is Joseph, who lags behind the procession in the temple, and turns his head in response to an angel who urges him to flee to Egypt (Fig. 125). The position of the angel is itself noteworthy. The curve of his suspended body unites the two episodes. Of his symmetrical wings, one points toward Egypt, the other toward Jerusalem, and each occupies another slab of the frieze.[131] The center implied in this division of the scenes is to the right of the column below and does not correspond to the midpoint of the frieze. But the direction of the Flight is opposed to that of the Magi below, and the Presentation is in corresponding opposition to the Holy Family. This chiasmic symmetry of separate groups is a typical mediaeval pattern, especially evident in ornament and color.

In reliefs of the Magi, the Annunciation and Visitation below this frieze (Figs. 122, 126, 127), the order of scenes is unequivocally from left to right as in western script. But on the west wall the direction is reversed. The banquet of Dives is represented at the right; the beggar lies at the left, is carried to heaven by an angel, and reposes in the bosom of Abraham at the end of the frieze (Figs. 121, 132, 133). In the central panels, the death of the rich man is at the right and his subsequent punishment at the left (Figs. 128, 130). In the lowest reliefs, of Unchastity and Avarice, which have no narrative connection, a sequence cannot be abstracted; but the scenes, together, form a symmetrical pair.

The contrast of the iconographic sequence on the two walls is, in an architectural sense, a symmetrical form. It is occasioned by the common relation of both walls to the portal; we shall grasp it more clearly if we imagine an open book in which the words of the right page run from left to right, and those of the left page from right to left.

The sequences described are not always in the dominant directions of the forms. The horizontals are primarily narrative, textual; the design of the larger reliefs of the porch is still close to the most archaic works of the cloister in the symmetry and isolation of scenes and even conflicts with the general succession in some details. Such a symmetry was inevitable in the Annunciation and the Visitation, or in the figures of Unchastity and the demon (Fig. 131). In the adjoining mutilated relief of the miser and the beggar, a devil, perched on the shoulders of the seated miser, prolongs the mass at the right in symmetrical opposition to the standing beggar (Fig. 128).

On the other hand, it should be observed that the legs of the demon and the unchaste woman, who form a balanced symmetrical group, have a common movement toward the right (north) in contrast to the narrative succession of scenes on the wall. By this means, perhaps, the pair is opposed to the Punishment of Avarice, in which the only moving figure, the beggar, is turned to the left (south). But on the relief of the Annunciation on the east wall (Fig. 126) both figures move toward the right (south), in contrast to the corresponding demon and the unchaste woman and in accord with the narrative sequence from left to right. In these panels the opposition of the turned heads and gestures modifies the simple parallelism of the movements of the limbs. It is apparent that the textual order of episodes does not determine uniquely the directions and order of forms but, as in the cloister, a more fundamental style of expression and design controls the distribution of scenes.

Fig. 123. Church; Detail of East Wall of Porch: Adoration of the Magi— Holy Family

Fig. 124.
Church; Detail
of East Wall of
Porch: Fall of the
Idols of He-
liopolis

On the east wall the Adoration of the Magi (Figs. 122, 123) is divided into two equal parts by the central column and the similar arches. A repeated wavy vertical contour unites the figures of the two groups. The Magi are not simply three equal figures in alignment, but the central is the tallest and stands under the highest lobe of the common trefoil, so that even here there is a distinction of central, axial, and lateral despite the direction of the Magi's movement and their common significance. In the Holy Family the Virgin is centralized, and the inequality of the Child and Joseph compensated by the introduction of the ox's head at the right.

The symmetry of such groups is primarily architectural or decorative; it has little expressive purpose as in the tympanum and certain capitals of the cloister.

It is a means of ordering a group, but does not impose a rigid form or correspondence on every detail. In this respect the later sculptures of Moissac approach Gothic composition. In the opposite reliefs of the Death and Punishment of Dives (Figs. 128, 129) a similar underlying formality of grouping may be observed in the agitated and varied movements of men and demons. But this formality is less apparent here than in the cloister or the tympanum. A more complex disorder is organized. The separate groups are extraordinarily restless and correspond in their zigzag and wavy movements to the asymmetrical, irregular architecture and to the highly emotional and dramatic conception of the subjects. Whole incidents are presented with a genrelike familiarity, and imaginative symbolical groups, like the punishments of vices, have the concreteness and mobility of an actual episode.

We can no longer judge of the character of the Annunciation which had been mutilated and was restored by a modern sculptor without understanding of Romanesque style; but in the Visitation is preserved for us a magnificent pantomime unparalleled in Romanesque representations of the scene (Fig. 127). Instead of the usual embrace of the two women, in which a sculptor of the cloister found a pattern of rigid lines, like the letter M (Fig. 66), or the traditional type of Elizabeth and Mary standing calmly separated in simple contemplation of each other, the sculptor of the porch has, by deep sympathy and by exploiting the dramatic force of every flection of the body, composed a new scene in which the emotion of the meeting and mutual revelation is expressed in both the gestures and the strange elongated zigzags of the pregnant women. This deliberate staccato rhythm is refined by numerous delicate lines formed by draperies of such thinness that the women appear most tenderly clothed and their bodies spiritual. One raises the edge of her veil or shawl to disclose a single breast in sign of motherhood; the left breast is covered by the hand turned palm outward in communication. The other woman inclines her head and indicates through the delicate cloth the swelling breast and nipple. The hands of both are thin and bony and the slender wrists are striated with the ridges of tendons.

Despite the mutilation of the faces, which probably had little expression, the feelings are adequately symbolized in the gestures and the structure of the bodies. Yet the simple zigzag of the limbs is not uniquely determined by the narrative; it carries also an expression independent of the meaning of the figures and common to scenes that represent other subjects.

What could be more remote from that maternal pair than the punishment of Unchastity? The figure of the loose woman tortured by toads and serpents (Fig. 131) has the posture of the Virgin of the Annunciation, and the horrible demon who pursues her repeats the gestures and flections of the left figure of the Visitation. But the legs of the demon parallel the legs of the woman as if they marched in a common procession. It is the elements of design and the typical forms that are the same in the two scenes. The wholes are different; and in the wholes are expressed the specific character of each subject, but with a common accent which is that of the entire portal and is imposed on no matter what incident or figure.

The death of the rich man is an enclosed picture in a modern sense, with a literal reproduction of the deathbed (Fig. 129). The haggard Dives is thinner, more bony than at his banquet table—his head resting on an inclined pillow, his scrawny breast uncovered, the body under a pleated blanket. His mourning wife kneels at the bedside just as the beggar Lazarus lay beside the table. The demons who descend to take his soul are described with an atrocious veracity. In the adjoining panel (Fig. 130) they trample on his fallen body weighted by the moneybag, and ride on a miserable woman with hanging breasts who emerges from the background in the middle of the field. By the almost chaotic, salient, curved and an-

Fig. 125. Church; Detail of East Wall of Porch: Flight into Egypt

115

gular, swarming masses throughout this sculpture, the ferocity and turbulence of the story are wonderfully expressed. But the effect inheres also in the completeness and detailed—even accurate—articulation of the monstrous demons. The extraordinary reality of these horrible, fantastic figures with animal parts—yet assimilated to a human structure—matches the unexpected precision with which the sculptors of the porch have represented on the capitals and modillions various morbid and deformed human heads. In the spandrel above the western reliefs is a leering old woman, with open, toothless mouth, stringy neck muscles and flying, disarranged hair (Fig. 147). Her eyes are barely open, as in extreme old age; her tongue lies weakly in the bottom of her mouth. Another head is of a goitrous woman grimacing in half-witted complacence (Fig. 131–right).

These human types are not required by the iconographic program and must therefore express an individual interest and initiative of the sculptor. But they are so common in French Romanesque art, especially in the decoration of modillions (Figs. 148–157), that they can hardly be ascribed to the curiosity of a single sculptor and must embody a common perception. They seem especially strange in an art which, in its monumental religious compositions, applies generalized forms and abstract geometrical combinations. Regarded in the light of the monstrous in other primitive arts, this contrast of abstraction and realism is

less surprising. The process of abstraction in Romanesque art includes an audacious distortion of ideal and symbolic figures for expressive ends; in the exact representation of monstrous, already deformed human heads, energy of expression was directly attained. The extremes of realism and abstraction have a common arbitrariness. The marginal position of the deformed heads in the decoration of a wall reflects their independence of an ideal or symbolic beauty. They are individuals who, in themselves, constitute the form of a "servile" architectural member—a corbel or modillion—which is a repeated minor element of construction, while the tympanum is a unique monument within the monument, an image of heaven erected above the entrance to the church.

The fantasy of Romanesque sculptors was more prolific in the creation of types of evil and violence than of beatitude. On the capital from which spring the two western arches we may see the demonic and human combined in a religious theme. The punishment of the damned is represented here. I suppose it is the association of this capital with the other scenes of punishment that led de Lasteyrie to describe the sculptures of the portal as a Last Judgment. A nude man and woman with bowed, repentant, suffering heads are tied by a rope held by an appalling devil. His whole body, from head to claws, is covered with thick scales. He has the curled snout of the monster on the lintel and a long, corrugated tongue which

Fig. 126. Church; Detail of East Wall of Porch: Annunciation

Fig. 127. Church; Detail of East Wall of Porch: Visitation

116

licks the tail of another nude demon. The latter is smooth-skinned but no less frightful in the knotted muscles, the tail ending in a serpent's head, and his own wolfish head in forked bristling hairs. He devours the left arm of a woman. In all these minutely rendered demons and human figures the forms and surfaces contribute to a common agitation. They resemble in this respect the composition of more ideal figures.

* * * * *

In the sculptures of the porch the construction of space undergoes a marked change from the methods of the cloister. Not only is space deepened by the overlapping of figures and by great differences of relief, but horizontal planes and architectural accessories are employed to realize this more extended depth. The upper surfaces of the beds of the Virgin and the dying rich man are rendered as horizontal planes (Figs. 123, 129). Only in the table of the feasting scene (Fig. 132) and in the pillow of Dives does a slight inclination recall the earlier archaic distortion. The feet of standing figures are more firmly planted on the deep base molding of each panel (but the slightly sloping surface of some of these bases [Fig. 131] indicates the persistence of the earlier conception). In the Adoration of the Magi, a column which separates the Magi from the Virgin and Christ stands in front of the field of relief rather than in it, while the main arches and subordinate trefoils, in lower relief than the figures, define a foreground and background architecture in space (Figs. 122, 123).

The cloister capital with the same subject (Fig. 36) enables us to study the change in representation in this short period. In the porch the space has been deepened by the addition of Joseph and the animals, with their overlapping masses and higher relief. The proportions of human beings and beasts are still arbitrary. The small size of the ox cannot be attributed to the sculptor's desire to suggest a great depth by a perspective diminution. Something of the superposed arrangement of the Magi's horses on the cloister capital survives in the placing of the ox and ass above the figures, although the traditional image of the Nativity assigned to them a similar position. The ox standing without support contradicts the framework of ground and background in the rest of the relief. Of the ass, the head alone is rendered; and this head is visible only if we view the sculpture from the left—it is carved in the spring of the arch and is partly concealed by the projecting capital.[132] This denial of the architectural frame makes the latter a part of the scene, but so inexplicable a part in its contradiction of the spatial unity that we must regard the penetration of the frame by the ass as an iconographic and technical expedient and as a correlate of the arbitrary, irregular architecture and the naive realism of the whole, rather than as an approach to an open, more extended image space. But this peculiarity is worth noting, for it is by such exigencies that more consistent spatial forms are later suggested.

Fig. 128. Church; Detail of West Wall of Porch: The Punishment of Avarice

Fig. 129. Church; Detail of West Wall of Porch: Death of Dives

Fig. 130. Church, Detail of West Wall of Porch: Hell Scene—Punishment of Avarice and Unchastity

More significant are the numerous overlappings that lead us in well-ordered sequence to the background. At the bottom of the relief are the legs of the Child, the bed cover, a fragment of the underlying sheet, the bed itself, and finally between these and the wall, the legs of Joseph and his seat. In the upper half the depth is more vigorously indicated; the body of the ox extends behind the Virgin and Christ, while his head is sharply turned, almost *en face*, and brought forward to a more prominent plane. The great thickness of the relief slab[133] permits a deep modeling of the profile torso and head of figures which are practically detached from the background, as on the tympanum. The left arm of Joseph, which was extended to reach the Virgin's elbow, was completely freed from the wall and has been broken. In the tympanum, however, such consistent choice of the profile of a torso is almost entirely lacking. It is limited there to one or two elders.

The representation of profiles is still archaic in that it depends on a thick slab which admits a carving of the farther side of the head in the round. The profile is not a perspective projection but the side of a head carved like a statue, with the whole face quite visible. The sculptor wishes to reproduce, as far as possible, the entire surface of an object, and to render his work intelligible from several points of view. Hence the lower parts of the body are nowhere in strict profile. The two legs are not permitted to overlap completely as in a perfectly profiled figure in nature. The axes of the legs deviate from the torso to produce a distinct view of each limb. The shoulders of the Magi are not perpendicular to the background as the strict profile of their heads and their movement would suggest, but are turned at an angle. Otherwise it would be necessary to foreshorten in order to compress the breadth of the shoulders within the narrower depth of relief; and foreshortening is still undeveloped in these early sculptures. The haloes are always carved flat against the wall and set behind the heads of the figures as if carried on the farther shoulder or applied to the concealed side of the face—a convention that persists up to the early Renaissance period. In a similar way, suspended or flying draperies covering no part of the figure are never represented perpendicular to the wall, but are expanded on a plane parallel to it.

These observations concerning the relief of the Magi apply equally to the others. In the death of Dives we see a similar arrangement of figures in front of and behind a bed (Fig. 128). Only here the pictorial unity is better established, for the group is self-contained and independent of the adjoining relief of the punishment. The kneeling wife before the bed and the horizontal plane of the reclining Dives are as effective in creating depth as the corresponding group on the opposite wall. The interception of the lower bodies of the demons by the bed, of the wings of one demon by the right frame, of the angel by clouds and the lobes of the trefoil arch, suggests a further space behind these figures. In the adjacent relief (Fig. 130) the nude bust of the unchaste woman emerges from the wall like a console ornament without indication of the rest of the figure. In the feast of Dives (Fig. 132) only the upper body of the servant is seen under an archway, while the body of the Virgin in the Presentation is partly obscured by Anna (?) and Simeon (Figs. 4, 5).

With all these approaches to a construction of space, it is nevertheless clear that the concept of a unified three-dimensional space in which figures act, bend, cross, and meet is foreign to the sculptor. This is obvious in the upper horizontal reliefs in which figures far from each other in time and place are grouped together as if in one scene. The continuous method does not preclude the organization of a consistent common space, as is apparent from Roman and Renaissance landscapes. But in Moissac the figures move before—or, rather, across—a changing background; on the same band we see Heliopolis and Jerusalem, or the interior of Dives' house and the tree

Fig. 131. Church; Detail of West Wall of Porch: The Punishment of Unchastity

Fig. 132. Church; Detail of West Wall of Porch: Dives

of Paradise. If the feet of the recumbent Lazarus and the dogs who lick his wounds are in the house of Dives, the beggar's head is already under the tree of Paradise (Fig. 121).

Even within a single scene, like the Banquet of Dives, despite the common architecture, each figure moves in a private space not consistently related to the larger planes of the whole (Figs. 132, 133). The servant, who seems to emerge from behind the table, is, with respect to the arch, nearer to us than Dives, whom he serves. This composite character of the whole space—the independent construction of each figure in depth—is better illustrated in the Presentation of Christ in the Temple (Fig. 4, 5). Simeon and Joseph are carved under arches, while the two women stand in front of the arches in a foreground plane. But so far is the sculptor from a conception of the space as distinct in shape, like any receptacle, that he has contradicted the implied order of planes for plastic fullness. One arm of the Virgin extends from behind Simeon who, with respect to the common architectural background, is behind the Virgin. By an even more remarkable reversal the nearest figure is the shortest, and the most distant one, Simeon, the tallest. This reversed perspective is to be distinguished from that of ancient Oriental and Early Christian art which sometimes placed large figures above or behind the smaller ones and aimed thereby to render concrete the differences in power or significance. In those earlier arts the reversal had spatial meaning because the position in an upper part of a scene denoted distance as well as a superior importance. In Moissac the difference of height is not hierarchal or only a perspective device; as already observed, it is a consistent element in an art which promotes contrasts in the effort to realize effects of movement and expression of excited energies. When we follow the rhythmical undulations of the contours of the figures in the scene discussed we arrive at the different heads without surprise at their inequality; its arbitrariness is dissolved in the pervasive movement to which the whole has been submitted.

Small details of the architecture reveal further the character of the style. The two arches of the Presentation are of unequal span, and are not rendered with the same completeness. The larger arch, at the right, is carried by capitals, while the other has no visible supports. The construction is lost behind the figures, and even where an unsculptured surface might admit some indication of a column or base (as between the feet of Simeon and the Virgin), it is not represented.

In the spandrels a central turret is flanked by two rectangular buildings which ramp along the arches. Their windows are slightly tilted, as if voussoirs of the turning arches. But more interesting is the interception of the buildings by the upper frame of the relief. The buildings seem to disappear under the heavy molding and to pass beyond. That this was designed rather than simply the incidental result of material constraints is evident from the successive shortening of the windows as they approach the frame and the adaptation of the whole group of buildings and the larger arches to the narrow surface under the frame. The intersection has an obvious spatial effect but it is also part of an untectonic composition in which such contrasts and overlappings are striking features.

In the single enclosed scenes, on the other hand, the architectural frames provide indications of foreground and background and define the limits of action. Various movements and overlappings confirm the depth therein created. But a consistent construction is lacking. In the relief of the Magi the animals are incredibly placed, while the ground plane does not accord in its depth with the space suggested above it. The same contradiction appears in the Death of Dives. The depth is not uniformly realized and the space lacks a clear configuration.

An approach to an enclosed or uniform space is evident in several details. The trefoil arches of the lower panels are not flat, but salient in plan, and support a gabled roof of three sloping sides which converge toward the vertical axis of the panel. The figures beneath seem to stand under a sloping canopy. A similar but more significant touch appears on the right side of the feast of Dives (Figs. 121, 132) in the chamfered vertical border converging toward the scene. Had another such wall been placed on the left, the whole interior would have been clearly defined and a symmetrical boxlike space, a uniformly deep receptacle of the other masses, would have resulted. But this solution, which implies a conception of space as an ideal regular form and artistic means, was not to come until much later, in the Gothic period.

Foreshortening is likewise more apparent than actual. The horizontal and vertical planes perpendicular to the wall are reproduced in their full depth rather than foreshortened. Lines converging toward a central point in the background are unknown. It was possible to arrange the folds of the bed so that they produced an effect of recession by means of their lines alone. But this was not admitted by the sculptor, though a matter of everyday observation. In the roof frame of the Visitation the convergence of the gable walls is contradicted by the absence of foreshortening in the receding windows. It is obvious that the sculptor conceived of all planes as equally distinct relief surfaces. Just as he turned to the side and carved the less visible surface of a head as if it were a statue in the round, he rendered with equal fidelity to fact, rather than perspective vision, the sides of buildings. In the city of Heliopolis (Fig. 124) which by its scale is a symbol of a city rather than a true background of the idols, the doorway (so small that the figures even by stooping could not enter it) is carved on a vertical plane perpendicular to the background and is invisible except to the approaching family. It is cut in the thickness of the relief. In the house of Dives a similar surface is slightly inclined, so that it appears foreshortened to the spectator, although carved without foreshortening (Fig. 132).

That the sculptor had some awareness of linear perspective is evident in his treatment of the left building of Heliopolis (Fig. 124). Having observed the convergence of the roof and ground lines of such structures, he has rendered the walls, windows, and roof as inclining toward the ground and has shown another side of the building at a much less obtuse angle than appears in the buildings of the cloister. But his representation is so far from accurate that we think of the inclination as the result less of a recession into depth than of a peculiar diagonal ground. Besides, the proportioning of the idols takes away all suggestion of verity from the perspective of the architecture.

Still another means of creating the effect of space is approached by the sculptor. To confirm the full solidity of the Magi's bodies, of which some parts are invisible, the inner sides of their mantles that envelop these parts are extended in very low relief across the background wall, so that they cast no shadow (Fig. 122). In the same way the star of the Magi (unlike the star in the cloister) is a barely visible petaled form on the trefoil arch above the Child (Fig. 123), while on the opposite wall the tree of Paradise (Figs. 121, 133) is carved in very slight relief as if far behind the figures. In these three examples the minimizing of relief is not occasioned by the thinness of the object alone or by other overlapping surfaces, but an attempt is made to suggest a distant plane or location by a limited salience and modeling.

The image of Heliopolis includes an extraordinary representation of an interior (Fig. 124). In many mediaeval and even early Renaissance paintings the front wall of a house is removed so that we may follow the action as if from within. In Moissac by a more complex dissection of the building, the anterior column and voussoirs of an arch seen in profile have been omitted, as in a cross-section in modern architectural drawing.

We may conclude from this study of the representation of groups of figures in Moissac that neither in the most archaic capitals of the cloister nor in the more elaborate and fully realized figures of the porch is there a clear abstraction of an enclosing space in which the figures move. But there is, on the other hand, an approach to the separate elements of such a space, manifest in the more realistic rendering of individual figures. The space as a whole is never presupposed as in later art, and we cannot, therefore, explain the various distortions and illogicalities of the works in Moissac as tentative solutions of a difficult problem or the attempts by an inferior culture to represent a complex idea. Actually, the idea of a regular, cubical space in art is very simple, but it is remote from the style of this period which coordinates separate figures in surface arabesques of intricate design. The subject matter demanded a grouping in depth, which was furthered by a growing skill in representation. But the depth resulted from the piece-meal construction of separate figures and accessories one by one. Most important for the later development is the gradual formation of horizontal planes and the construction of architectural frames so salient that the relief seems enclosed and its figures more deeply set within. Beyond such devices the depth is achieved, not by foreshortening, but by a scale reproduction of the actual mass of the object.

* * * * *

In the construction and surface of this mass the sculptures of the porch have been developed beyond the tympanum in the direction already intimated in the change from the styles of the cloister to that of the tympanum. The figures are still more detached from the background and are more plastic, not merely in the sense that their relief is higher, but that the bodies are more richly molded and the surfaces of drapery more deeply and complexly grooved. The figures stand, bend, and turn more freely within their narrow space. If they are still limited by a rigid conception of the axes, they are nevertheless much freer than in the cloister and tympanum.

The change is not uniform or equally evident in all the sculptures of the porch, for two distinct hands were at work here. The growth beyond the style of the

*Fig. 133.
Church; Detail
of West Wall of
Porch: Angel
carries soul of
beggar Lazarus*

tympanum is more evident in the large reliefs than in the horizontal friezes. The latter are the works of another master with a distinct character, apparent not only in the forms and design of his panels but in the very type and expression of his figures. The individual heads and drapery forms reproduce with a considerable fidelity motifs of the tympanum. The patriarch Abraham (Fig. 134) has the long beard and the flowing locks of Christ, and like him is seated frontally on a great cushioned throne (Fig. 101). His halo is richly jeweled, and the lower edges of his garment are broken by two flaring fanlike pleatings, as on the figure of Christ. The angels' heads are close replicas of the symbol of Matthew. The ass of the Flight (Fig. 120) is short-legged like the lion and the bull (Figs. 113,

114). The details of drapery are too obviously like those of the elders to require an extensive comparison. But the following differences may be noted. The multiplying of pleats and breaks is less elaborate in the friezes than in the tympanum and far less imaginative in line. The lower folds of Christ and Abraham illustrate the difference very clearly. With the exception of two examples, on the leg of the Infant in the Presentation, the doubled fold is absent from the upper zone of reliefs. But this fold was only infrequently applied on the tympanum itself, and mainly on the taller figures. There is one detail of costume that is unknown in the earlier work. The collars of Dives (Fig. 132) and the Infant Christ in the Flight into Egypt (Fig. 125) are fastened under the chin and folded at the sides to form lapels.

The modeling of the heads and the bodies, though apparently as on the tympanum, produces softer, more rounded surfaces and lacks the sharp meeting of planes which accents the quadrature of surfaces in the earlier sculpture.

In the scene of the Presentation the heads are carved with a characteristic expression of feeling that does not appear in the reliefs below. The brows are lifted high, the eyes are wide open and the mouth turned at the corners in a faint smile. In the head of Joseph the effect is one of anxiety, in the others, of joy (Figs. 4, 5). In all of them the resemblance to the eager Matthew symbol of the tympanum is evident. The bent legs of the figures and the curved or zigzag contours increase the effect of excitement. The opposite relief of Lazarus and Dives is calmer and the figures are less animated. There the vertical and horizontal scaffolding of the design accords with the placidity of facial expression (Fig. 132). It is only in the group of the recumbent Lazarus and the angel, which departs from the regular scheme of the adjoining figures in its diagonal lines, that we find something of the gesture and facial movement of the Presentation.

The shortness of these figures is not an obvious peculiarity of the style as one might suppose from the contrast with the elongated Magi and Virgin below. A similar difference of proportions appears in the lower row of elders and the seraphim under similar conditions of design within a single work. The sculptors have in each case freely adapted the figures to the height of the relief. A similar duality in canons of proportions of small and large figures has been demonstrated in other schools of French Romanesque sculpture by Laran.[134] But in the upper friezes of the porch the figures are short not merely because of the scale and the narrow horizontal field; they have clumsier, heavier bodies than the corresponding elders. The squatness of the figures pertains also to the domestic and genre realism of the sculptor, just as the elongation of Christ and the seraphim on the tympanum has a religious dignity, formally accentuated in a style of intense, imaginative linear movement. In the scenes of banqueting on the capitals of the cloister no figure is represented actually eating, with food at the mouth, like the rich wife in the upper frieze of the porch (Fig. 132). She recalls Germanic art of the later Middle Ages.[135] Nor is Lazarus in the cloister (Fig. 67) so unmistakably a dying beggar as the clumsy, sore-covered figure in the porch.[136]

The master of the larger porch reliefs was a more skillful and original artist. He derives as obviously as his associate from the art of the tympanum master. But he has modified the style of the latter much more freely. His figures are even more slender and elongated, their garments are of thinner stuff, the folds arranged in more novel combinations, the heads modeled in greater detail. There is likewise in the work of this master a greater freedom in the movements of the figures. A comparison of the two figures of the Visitation with the two seraphim of the vision, who are so similar in pose, will make clear the difference between the style of the tympanum and its development on the porch. The marble material of the Visitation may be a factor in the greater delicacy of its surfaces; but this is something I cannot decide. Whereas in the tympanum all folds are lines inscribed on flat or broad, smoothly rounded surfaces, and regular pleatings are repeated in simple ornamental schemes, more plastic forms appear on these figures of the porch. The sleeves of the two women are casual, ungeometric pouches, broken by irregular folds. The section varies from fold to fold and is curved rather than rectilinear. Also, the concentric alternating lap folds which copy those of the right seraph are incised on a deeper concave surface. The double-incised forms are applied as on the tympanum, but are less insistently concentric and pronounced. The zigzag and meander contours of drapery, while they repeat the forms of the tympanum, are smaller in proportion to the whole figure, and in places, as at the lower edges of a garment, are more closely serried. On the

Fig. 134. Church; Detail of West Wall of Porch: Lazarus in Abraham's Bosom

123

abdomens of the two figures are small rippling grooves that appear also on Joseph and Simeon in the Presentation (Fig. 4, 5). They are unknown on the tympanum, but are suggested there by a more prominent and vigorous furrowing of the belly folds of the upper elder next to the right seraph (Fig. 103).

Another detail of the style of the tympanum that is more extensively used on the porch is the flying, fanlike fold attached to a long curved stem, as at the left leg of Christ (Fig. 101). On the porch it appears in

Fig. 135. Church; Detail of Portal: Peter and Paul below spring of archivolt.

the garments of the Magi, flattened against the wall, and on Isaiah, Peter, and Elizabeth (Figs. 136, 137, 127). In the last the lower edge of the tunic is broken by a smooth domical fold with patterned, zigzag opening, as in several of the elders. But it differs from the latters' in the position between the feet and in the detachment from a stem.

Of one fold on the later figures there is no intimation in the tympanum. On the right leg of Peter (Fig. 136) and the left of Isaiah (Fig. 137), above the knee, are incised two lines forming an angle of forty-five degrees. On Isaiah's leg it is repeated to form a chevron pattern. The same convention occurs also on the three Magi (Fig. 122).

The modeling of the figures refines and elaborates the forms of the tympanum. This is especially apparent in the hands, which are more delicate, and in the wrists, of which the tendons are indicated by slight striations. The vigorous and clearly blocked-out forms of the vision are replaced by more delicate and flowing surfaces. Compare the head of Peter (Fig. 136) with that of any figure on the tympanum and the greater search for surface variety and movement in the details of the first will be evident. The sculptor has renounced the elaborate locks and beards of the tympanum; but while retaining the archaic system of parallel striations and repeated locks of hair, he has introduced more curved lines. The moustache is not formed as before by hairs parallel to its long contours, but by spiral strands. Spiral and crocket ends appear already in the tympanum, but in the porch they are more common and less regular.

In the nude figure of the unchaste woman (Fig. 131) we may judge of the change in the sculpture of Moissac since the carving of the cloister capitals. The expressive contrast of the movements of her head and legs has already been noted on the capitals. But if the earlier sculptors chose to shorten the figure, the later artist has increased elongation to inhuman proportions. He has extended his observation to numerous details which escaped his predecessor, and created a nude female figure so elaborate in contour and surface beside the simpler nudes of the cloister, and so unforgettably expressive, that were it not in its present context we should not readily judge it to be a work of the early twelfth century. A similar nude figure of Luxuria at Charlieu also seems strangely precocious at this time in its massive articulation and fluent contours. In Moissac the Romanesque character is evident in the thoroughly symmetrical torso of the twisted figure, her parallel raised hands and pendant

Fig. 136.
Church; Detail
of Portal: St. Pe-
ter on West Jamb

Fig. 137.
Church; Detail
of Portal: Isaiah
on East Jamb

Fig. 138.
Church; Detail
of Narthex:
Capital of
Narthex

breasts, and the regular design of the suckling serpents. At the base of this vigorous plastic structure,
the toad who devours her sexual parts is enclosed by
her thighs and the hanging bodies of the serpents,
which unite with the torso to form a beautiful symmetrical scheme of fluent lines and bosses. The head is
mutilated, but enough remains for us to observe that
the sculptor produced features appropriate to the
theme and achieved an extraordinary realism. The
inclined head and wavy locks spread out on the breast
and shoulders are in themselves an impressive sculpture.

THE DOORPOSTS

The hand of the same master appears also in the
figures of Peter and Isaiah on the walls that support
the tympanum (Figs. 136, 137). They are of
almost identical size but are placed at unequal dis-
tances from the ground and from the scalloped edges
of the jambs. Peter is higher than Isaiah and not so
close to the door. This inequality is consistent with
the unequal breadth of the jambs and of the two
doorways; it entails an irregular, asymmetrical relation of the figures to the adjoining cusps. That these
irregularities were designed is evident from the measurements of the figures and the surrounding architecture. For the left jamb and doorway are together equal
to the right jamb and doorway, which are respectively
smaller and larger than the corresponding parts on
the other side.[136a] There can be no question, then,
considering the precise equality of the two halves of

the portal and the identical structure of the halves,
that the alternating variations were preconceived,
and were features of style rather than accidents of
work.

The extremities of the figures correspond to no
moldings or prominent architectural divisions. They
are thoroughly unarchitectural applications, independent of the structure of the wall. There are, however,
in the contours of the two figures analogies to the
scalloped profile of the jambs, but these contours are
conceived as contrasting lines and are subordinate to
diagonal schemes. It is characteristic of the style that
the contour of Peter's right side, which is a symmetrical counterpart, not repetition, of the scalloped
jamb, should be attached to a vertical colonnette. In
one sense the architecture may be considered subordinate to the sculpture, since the abnormal profile of
the jamb is justified by the movement of the figure
rather than the latter by the jamb.[137] The aesthetic
effect and specific religious expression presuppose this
autonomy of the plastic. On the west portal of
Chartres the elongation of the ancestors of Christ is a
human paraphrase of slender architectural verticals
though not determined by them; in Moissac, the
elongated Peter is an unstable figure without an axis
or a frame.

This Peter is an ascetic hardly expressive of the
Roman authority embodied in his name. The lion on
which he treads is barely observable beneath his feet.
The keys are sculptured to form the letters of his
monogram, but the tapering left hand is raised palm
outward beside it in more humble deference and in
contrasting diagonal movement. His left leg is a harsh
diagonal of unexpected rigidity, accented by the
hanging mantle folds that seem ruled mechanically
on the stone. The head, almost wrenched from the
shoulders in its marked inclination toward the doorway, forms a contrasting diagonal, while both movements are resumed in the zigzag of the bent right leg
on the other side. This opposition of limbs is the
underlying motif that makes the figure so intensely
expressive. The extreme slenderness of Peter, the ten-
uous, insecurely balanced figure, the striving of the
parts in different directions, the head one way, the
legs another, the hands and arms in similar disarray,
are all relevant to one idea, apparent in the head
itself. But the head (Fig. 136) shows less of the gaunt-
ness and ascetic nature, the painfully achieved, almost reluctant, spiritual submission that we sense in
the whole. And it may be said that here the expression of character is lodged primarily in the forms.

Fig. 139.
Church; Detail
of Narthex:
View from Inte-
rior of Narthex

Comparison of the saint and the left seraph on the tympanum (Fig. 110) will make clearer the nature of the forms of Peter which contribute to his powerful expressiveness. In the seraph the similar gestures and elongations are of quite different effect, for contrast is not so thoroughly sustained. His bent legs are parallel to each other. In Peter the right is bent, the left is extended stiffly in the opposite direction, and the feet are parted in further contrast, while in the seraph only one foot is carved, so that less opposition of line is possible. The lion's book and paws at this point only parallel the legs of the seraph and prolong their movement. The wings of the beast sweep across the field, connecting the lines of the seraph's body with other figures. But Peter is isolated, independent of others who might diminish the forcefulness of his own gestures, or reduce them to parts of a larger scheme. In the seraph there is a dominant inclination or turn of the figure toward Christ; but in Peter two directions struggle for dominance, the head and upper body toward the doorway or axis of the portal, the legs away from it. A long pleat flies from between the legs and issues in a suspended fold, outside the body contour, on the column that bounds the movement of the figure on the left. The tilt of Peter's head, as already observed, is sharp and agonized as if the muscles of the neck were stretched by this gesture. The head looks down rather than directly beyond like the seraph's.[138]

The difference between the two conceptions may be illustrated in the surfaces of the figures. In the seraph the limbs are equally salient. In Peter this simple treatment of the relief is changed only slightly, but with great effect. The section of the seraph's body is at almost all levels a symmetrical contour; in Peter it is more bulging or convex, in some places at the left, in others at the right. The knees are not in equal relief. Even the lion under Peter's feet projects farther at the left than the right. The greatest recession toward the background is at the waist. A similar effect appears on the angel of Matthew in the tympanum.

In the Isaiah, on the other jamb, the forms are essentially the same. But the contrasting directions of the head and legs are the simple Romanesque formula of the cloister and the porch, without the inspired accentuation in Peter. Isaiah's legs are turned toward the reliefs of the porch which fulfill the prophecy inscribed on his scroll; but his head is turned away from the scroll and these reliefs. The internal contrast is not an expression of a conflict within the man, but a purely formal conception that we have already

Fig. 140.
Church; Detail
of Portal: Tru-
meau

observed in other contexts, with an expressive force independent of the prophet-subject. In Isaiah the suspended scroll is a vertical band that indicates the axis from which this less animated figure bends. Perhaps the precise iconographic content, evident in the large inscription and the nearby associated themes of the Virgin limited the movement of the figure. In Souillac the marvelous Isaiah, carved by a sculptor of the same school, carries a great scroll inscribed only with his name. Perhaps it was in subordination to Peter, the patron of Moissac, that the prophet was restrained and his movement limited to a conventional form. The unequal breadth of the two jambs and the balanced inequality of the doorways imply the difference or contrast of the corresponding figures.

In the miniature figures of Peter and Paul surmounting the vertical bands of plants and birds on the beveled jambs framing the outer eastern colonnette, the contrast is more explicit and quaint. In chiasmic opposition to the larger Peter of the left doorpost and Paul on the west side of the trumeau, the little Paul is seated on the left jamb, while Peter sits inverted on the right. I have been taught that such small anomalies of design were a superstitious concession to the evil eye which detested nothing so much as a perfect craftsman. But in this instance contrast has become a rule, and in the literal inversion of the patron saint, who was martyred on the cross upside down, the assistant sculptor has appeased the devil and carried to a perfect but comic conclusion the conscious formulation of his master's style.[139]

THE TRUMEAU

I have not described the trumeau after the lintel, despite their architectural connection, because its sculpture is not a part of the original design. That a trumeau always stood here is evident from the structure of the tympanum and the lintel; but that the present one was sculptured at the same time as the stones above is less likely. Its carving is probably even later than the figures of the jambs and the side walls of the porch. The divergence from the rest of the portal may be seen not only in the style of its figured and animal decoration, but in the moldings and foliate ornament as well.

The section of the side jambs is fifty-three centimeters in depth, of the trumeau, forty-nine. Their profiles also differ (Fig. 139). In both trumeau and jambs a festooned, or lobed, colonnette is engaged to the sides facing the entrance-ways. On the trumeau it is segmental, and set between angular prismatic moldings that form a zigzag interrupted by the central colonnette; on the jambs it is of semicircular section and is placed on a flat band with outer chamfers. The trumeau has five scallops on each side, the jambs but four.[140] Their base moldings are also different.[141] The original impost of the trumeau has been replaced in recent times by an uncarved block of limestone unlike the marble of the block below. The capitals of the engaged colonnettes have been preserved and show a structure and foliate ornament resembling the capitals of the Romanesque windows of the church and several of the adjoining tower, but in contrast to the deeply undercut plant and animal forms of the other capitals of the porch and the portal.

The trumeau was already singled out for special admiration in the fourteenth century (Fig. 140). The abbot Aymeric de Peyrac then wrote that this stone and the marble font of the cloister (now destroyed) were "reputed the most beautiful, and the most subtly wrought, and were said to have been brought here with great cost and labor and even supposed to have been made miraculously rather than by a man, especially a simple abbot."[142]

It is a marble monolith, 3.52 meters high and about .72 wide. On its outer face are carved three

Fig. 141. Church; Detail of Trumeau: Head of a Prophet

superposed couples of crossed animals (Fig. 140). They are lion and lioness, contrary to the common description of them as male alone. The outer animal is always a lioness, alternating in direction from pair to pair. The beasts are mounted on each other's haunches, while their tails, distinguished by a smooth carrotlike termination in the female and by a similar form with a pebbled surface and a hooked end and lobed calyx envelope in the male, are interlaced between them on a background of acanthus rosettes.

On the sides of the trumeau are the elongated figures of Paul and a bearded prophet, engaged to curved colonnettes which terminate in a palmette capital on one side and an acanthus capital on the other (Figs. 142, 143, 144). The prophet stands with legs crossed, Paul with a simpler bending of the limbs. They are compressed within the narrow frame formed by the fore and rear parts of the animals and the back of the pillar, festooned like the jambs beside it. A series of imbricated semicircular scales, which Aymeric thought was the signature of the abbot Ansquitilius (1085–1115), decorates the back.

The sculptures are unarchitectural in effect, and betray no effort to accent the static function of the pillar. But this indifference to physical structure is consistent with the form of the trumeau, since the latter has itself been designed without regard to the expression of its function and even contradicts it. It contains hardly a vertical line. Its contours are scalloped both in elevation and plan; the colonnettes of its narrow sides are curved behind the figures engaged to them. The diagonal crossing of the lions throws the plastic accent on recurrent heads and legs along the broken edges of the trumeau. The vertical axis becomes plastically subordinate, even neutral, with the addition of circular rosettes behind the beasts. The placing of the figures, on the less visible narrow sides, is also significant of the unarchitectonic character of the style. But the positive energy and movement of the tympanum and porch, which imply these willful asymmetries, these irregular forms and contrasts of the trumeau, are less apparent in the latter.

Mâle has remarked of the animals that they are more Assyrian than the Assyrian lions themselves.[143] They are inferior copies of the symbol of Mark on the tympanum. They have the same peculiar muzzles, worried brows, short legs, and conventionalized locks of hair but lack the energy and powerful modeling of their original. Their caterpillar bodies are surcharged with the repeated ornamental details which formed a simple fringe in the tympanum. In this fantastic,

though not untraditional rearrangement of the usual portal lions, they have lost their ferocity. The threat of their animal bodies is diminished by their repeated pairing and crossing, the knotting of their tails, and the attachment to disks of foliage. The force of the diagonal movement of the beasts has been dissipated into a simple pattern and neutralized in their vertical succession. Lions are more effectively crossed on a capital of the narthex where the contours of the beasts are sharply isolated and intersect in rigorous correspondence with the enclosing volutes.

The rosettes carved on the outer surface of the pillar, as backgrounds of the crossed animals, are weak imitations of the forms of the lintel. The interspaces have been left bare, the cable omitted, the central knob treated like a button without the crispness or variety of the original, and the leaves themselves have been reduced to smaller, softer patterns, consisting of five spoon-grooved lobes. The eyelets are no longer effective in the design.

In the figures of the trumeau there is an analogous dilution of the powerful forms of the tympanum. They are even more slender than the figures of the porch, but their elongation is no longer a support of intense diagonal contrasts. It is an elegant proportion in figures whose movements are languid, almost indolent, versions of their prototypes.[144] A similar change is evident in the smoothly undulating surfaces of the heads and beards and the boneless hands (Fig. 144). The draperies have the thinness of certain Renaissance costumes. The doubled fold has been abandoned for more plastic, delicate forms.[145]

If the figures are not adapted to a caryatid function or designed in columnar forms, they are hardly troubled by the jagged, constraining structure in which they have been embedded. In neither figure does the compression between cusped edges and lions correspond to an inward involvement or sustained constriction and conflict of forms, or even the abstraction of vertical themes. They recall certain kings with legs crossed, engaged to the columns of St.-Denis and Chartres, more than their own prototypes in Aquitaine. Only the unarchitectural design of the trumeau has concealed this similarity.

THE ABBOT ROGER AND "ST. BENEDICT"

These two figures, placed high upon the capitals of columns engaged to the south wall of the porch, are themselves independent of the latter (Figs. 145, 146). They are not carved in the wall or even in a salient block which forms an essential part of it, as we might suppose from the engagement of the column, but are almost detached in high relief on a thick slab set into the wall subsequent to the construction. The background is, in fact, cut (like a flat pilaster) in slight salience from the wall. This separate relief background illustrates at the same time the independence of architecture already analyzed in the sculptures below, and also the persistence of an earlier method of relief even in figures which by their salience suggest a complete detachment from the background. The two figures exist in a space more emphatically defined than any we have seen below. Their feet are firmly planted on a deep, horizontal ground and are exaggerated in mass and flatness, as if to underline the newly achieved stance in space. On the trumeau, the feet of the prophet (Fig. 142) are still suspended in the archaic manner of the cloister, and on the jamb, Isaiah stands upon a sloping ledge (Fig. 137). Another horizontal surface confirms the depth of the figures on the columns; it is the slab above their heads, which was probably designed to protect them but serves also to mark the depth or projection of the stage on which they stand. In the description of the capitals of the cloister an analogous effect was observed in the projecting console above the head of Nebuchadnezzar (Fig. 74); but there the salience was slight and the corresponding ground plane still undeveloped.

The postures of the two figures also imply a development of spatial forms. By their religious office and significance they are bound to a frontal position and an ideal repose, like the abbot Durand in the cloister (Fig. 13); but the abbot Roger looks up to the left and the head and shoulders of St. Benedict are turned toward the right, although their glance has no perceptible object. If we compare them with the opposed apostles on a single pier of the cloister (Figs. 6, 18) whose heads are turned to each other, we see that the more recent figures are less bound to the wall and that their arms, if parallel to the wall, are less constrained by this archaic procedure. The immobility of the two men contrasts with the figures of the tympanum, as if by this liberation of the mass all the energy of line had been sacrificed. But this iconlike immobility is distinct from the stiffness of the apostles in the cloister, which was an unnatural, imposed rigidity, whereas Benedict stands humbly with an ascetic quietude and detachment and the physically mediocre Roger, in his massive pyramidal costume, has an air of energy and assertion. They are portraits of contemporary monastic figures of the contemplative and active life.

The dominance of the mass of the figures is a further development of the style of the porch. Instead of a complicated course of pleatings at the edges of the costume, the sculptor has accented the larger, plastic undulation of the mass of the garment about the legs. In Benedict the folds are simpler, softer, more natural forms; the sleeves are deeply hollowed to expose the ends of an inner garment. The contours of both figures have been simplified and rounded to produce a clearer, more definite solid.

Despite this simplification and immobility, the characters of the earlier style persist to some degree in the two figures. Roger is placed to the left of the slab rather than in the exact center like Durand, and his name, BEA(tu)S ROT(g)ERIUS ABBAS, is inscribed at the right. If he wears the symmetrical costume of an abbot, it is no longer disposed in its ideal or typical order but is stirred by an accidental asymmetry of the parts. The turn of the abbot's head is contrary to the inclination of his staff. The authoritative hand is not rigidly parallel to the background like his predecessor's but is bent back in a more natural gesture. The ascending diagonal lines of his costume are crossed by other angular forms. Large, vigorous pleats are placed asymmetrically on the lower edge. In Roger we see a realistic asymmetry imposed on an iconographically symmetrical object, as in Durand an inherent symmetry was reproduced with an effect of intricate abstract ornament.

Benedict is a slightly taller, more slender figure than Roger, but no more closely related to the earlier reliefs of the porch. The two figures are so different in expression that it is difficult at first to see their common authorship. This difference attests the development of the style in which one could conceive such individual interpretations of a historical and an almost contemporary figure.

There are no figures below quite like them, but their forms suggest either a later work of the master of the horizontal friezes of the porch or of a sculptor closely related to him. The more recent date is evident in purely material details like the relation of the slabs of these figures to the surrounding wall, as well as in the plastic development of the figures. The modeling and perspective of the hands and sleeves of Benedict is of a naturalism beyond that of the lower porch reliefs. The inscription beside Roger has larger, rounder, more plastic letters than the inscription of Isaiah (Fig. 137). The forms of A and R are especially noteworthy in their approach to early Gothic majuscules.

Fig. 145. Church; Detail of Exterior of Porch: St. Benedict (?) on West Column

Fig. 146. Church; Detail of Exterior of Porch: Abbot Roger (1115–1131) on East Column

NOTES

1. This work is the first part of a doctor's dissertation accepted by the Faculty of Philosophy of Columbia University in May, 1929 and published with many corrections in *The Art Bulletin* (XIII, pp. 248–351, 464–531). The corrected text was reprinted in my *Selected Papers, I, Romanesque Art*, New York, Braziller, 1977, pp. 131–264. In that reprint, it was not possible for me, except in a few places, to add references to more recent literature. Those additions and new comments are enclosed in brackets. The present reprint reproduces the text of 1977, with a new set of illustrations from photographs by David Finn.

I have profited by the generosity of Professor Porter, who opened his great collection of photographs to me, and by the criticism of Professor Morey. I have been aided also by the facilities and courtesy of the Frick Reference Library, the Pierpont Morgan Library, and the Avery and Fine Arts Libraries of Columbia University.

I owe a special debt to the late Monsieur Jules Momméja of Moissac, who taught me much concerning the traditions of the region, and to the late Monsieur Dugué, the keeper of the cloister of Moissac, who in his very old age and infirmity took the trouble to instruct me. He permitted me to study the unpublished plans of the excavations of the church, made in 1902.

I must thank, finally, the Carnegie Corporation of New York, which supported my graduate studies at Columbia University, and enabled me by its grant of a fellowship in 1926–1927 to travel for sixteen months in Europe and the Near East.

2. Emanuel Löwy, *The Rendering of Nature in Greek Art*. English translation, London, Duckworth, 1907.

3. Devals, *Les voies antiques du département de Tarn-et-Garonne*, in *Bulletin Archéologique de la Soc. Archéol. de Tarn-et-Garonne*, Montauban, 1872, p. 360.

4. Dumège, *Antiquités de la ville de Moissac* (manuscript copy in the Hotel-de-Ville of Moissac), 1823, pp. 1 ff., 127 ff., 140 ff. See also *Bull. Archéol. de la Soc. Archéol. de Tarn-et-Garonne*, LI, 1925, pp. 140, 141, for a report of the discovery of Roman bricks of the year 76 B.C. under an old house in Moissac. The presence of Roman remains was observed by the abbot Aymeric de Peyrac in his chronicle, written c. 1400 (Paris, Bibl. Nat. ms. latin 4991-A, f. 154 r, col. I)—*Denique in multis locis harum parcium in agris et viis publicis apparent antiqua pavimenta que faciunt intersigna villarum antiquarum et penitus destructarum.* . . .

5. A. Lagrèze-Fossat, *Études historiques sur Moissac*, Paris, Dumoulin, III, 1874, pp. 8 ff. and 495–498, and E. Rupin, *L'abbaye et les cloîtres de Moissac*, Paris, Picard, 1897, pp. 21–25, for a *résumé* of the evidence concerning the period of foundation and the various local legends which pertain to it.

6. Rupin, *loc. cit.*

7. *La Vie de St. Didier, Évêque de Cahors* (630–655), edited by Poupardin, Paris, Picard, 1900, pp. 22 ff. This biography was written in the late eighth or early ninth century by a monk of Cahors who utilized a source contemporary with the saint. One of the manuscripts comes from Moissac (Bibl. Natl. lat. 17002).

8. Rupin, *op. cit.*, pp. 28, 29.

9. On these disasters and the submission to Cluny, see Rupin, *op. cit.*, pp. 31–50.

10. An inscription of the period, now enwalled in the choir of the church, records the event. Rupin, *op. cit.*, pp. 50–52, and fig. 5.

11. Rupin, *op. cit.*, pp. 57–62.

12. *Ibid.*, pp. 62, 63.

13. Paris, Bibl. Nat. ms. latin 4991-A, f. 160 vo., col. I. The text is published by Rupin, *op. cit.*, p. 66, n. 2 and by V. Mortet, *Recueil de textes relatifs à l'histoire de l'architecture en France au moyen-âge. XIe-XIIe siècles*, Paris, Picard, 1911, pp. 146–148. The construction of the cloister by Anquêtil is also indicated by an inscription of the year 1100 in the cloister. For a photograph see Fig. 3.

14. Rupin, *op. cit.*, p. 350, and Mortet, *op. cit.*, p. 147. Aymeric mentions a "very subtle and beautiful figure in the shrine in the chapel of the church" made for Hunaud, and similar works in the priory of Layrac, near Agen, which belonged to Moissac.

15. Rupin, *op. cit.*, pp. 70–75. The portrait of Roger is sculptured on the exterior of the south porch (see below, Fig. 137). The evidence for the attribution of the domed church to Roger, presented in the last chapter of my dissertation (1929), is published in my article on the sculpture of Souillac. See *Selected Papers, I, Romanesque Sculpture*, 1977, pp. 129–130, n. 4.

16. Rupin, *op. cit.*, pp. 181 ff., has listed the property of the abbey, and reproduced a map (opposite p. 181) showing the distribution of its priories and lands.

Fig. 147. Church; Detail of Portal: Head of Grimacing Woman

Fig. 148–156. Church; Detail of Exterior: Modillions of West Tower

17. *Millénaire de Cluny*, Macon, 1910, II, pp. 30, 31, and Pignot, *Historie de l'ordre de Cluny*, II, pp. 190 ff.

18. G. M. Dreves, *Hymnarius Moissiacensis. Das Hymnar der Abtei Moissac im 10. Jahrhundert nach einer Handschrift der Rossiana.* *Analecta Hymnica Medii Aevi,* II, Leipzig, 1888, and C. Daux, *L'Hymnaire de l'abbaye de Moissac aux X-XI ss.,* Montauban, 1899.

The remnants of the mediaeval library of Moissac were brought to Paris in the seventeenth century by Foucault, and are now preserved in the Bibliothèque Nationale. They are mainly religious texts. For their history and content, and for ancient catalogues of the library of Moissac, see L. Delisle, *Le Cabinet des Manuscrits,* I, pp. 457–459, 518–524.

19. They were called to the attention of scholars by Delisle more than forty-five years ago, but have never been published as a group.

20. Rupin, *op. cit.,* pp. 82, 83.

21. *Ibid.,* pp. 86 ff.

22. *Ibid,* pp. 107, 354 ff.

23. *Ibid,* p. 345.

24. Except for the angel of the Annunciation on the south porch and several modillions. On the fortunes of the abbey building in the nineteenth century, see Lagrèze-Fossat, *op. cit.,* III, pp. 266–268,

25. Rupin, *op. cit.,* p. 66, n. 2, and Mortet, *op. cit.,* pp. 147, 148.

26. *Ibid.*

27. He writes, "*Credo quod ipse (Asquilinus) fecerit scribi etiam in lapide et de eisdem litteris consecrationis monasterii facte de tempore domini Durandi abbatis.*" See Mortet, *op. cit.,* p. 148.

28. Mortet, *op. cit.,* pp. 146, 147.

29. Léon Godefroy, a canon of the church of St. Martin in Montpézat (Tarn-et-Garonne), visited Moissac about 1645. He observed numerous relics in the treasure, including the body of St. Cyprian. Mosaics covered the entire floor of the church. He paid little attention to the portal and said of the cloister that it was "*fort beau ayant de larges galeries et le préau environné d'un rebord . . . colonnes d'un marbre bastard . . . et des statues qui représentent les Apostres. Si ces pièces sont mal faites il faut pardonner à la grossièreté du temps qui ne possédoit pas l'art de la sculpture au point qu'on fait à present.*" He observed also a fountain in one corner of the cloister.

See Louis Batcave, *Voyages de Léon Godefroy en Gascogne, Bigorre et Béarn (1644–1646),* in *Études Historiques et Religieuses du diocèse de Bayonne,* Pau, VIII, 1899, pp. 28, 29, 73, 74.

30. *Gallia Christiana,* 1st ed., 1656, IV, pp. 678–680; 2nd ed., 1715, I, pp. 157–172.

31. Rupin, *op. cit.,* p. 6.

32. Delisle, *op. cit.*

33. F. Pottier, in *Bull. de la Soc. Archéol. de Tarn-et-Garonne,* 1888, p. 67.

34. *Antiquités de la Ville de Moissac,* 1823. The copy in Moissac is kept in the archives of the Hôtel-de-Ville.

35. Nodier, Taylor, and de Cailleux, *Voyages pittoresques et romantiques dans l'ancienne France,* Languedoc I, partie 2, Paris, 1834.

36. Jules Marion, *L'abbaye de Moissac,* in *Bibliothèque de l'École des Chartes,* 3e série, I, 1849, pp. 89–147, and in the same journal, *Notes d'un voyage archéologique dans le sudouest de la France.* 1852, pp. 58–120.

37. Paris, 1854–1869, III, pp. 283-285; VII, pp. 289–293, etc.

38. *Études Historiques sur Moissac,* Paris, Dumoulin, 3 volumes, 1870, 1872, 1874. The archaeological study is in the third volume.

39. J. Mignot, *Recherches sur la chapelle de St. Julien,* in *Bull. de la Soc. Archéol. de Tarn-et-Garonne,* IX, 1881, pp. 81–100; and *Recherches sur les constructions carlovingiennes à Moissac,* ibid, XI, 1883, pp. 97–105. Henry Calhiat, *Le tombeau de Saint Raymond à Moissac,* ibid, I, 1869, pp. 113–117. Chadruc de Crazannes, *Lettre sur une inscription commémorative de la dédicace de l'église des Bénédictins de Moissac,* in *Bulletin Monumental,* VIII, 1852, pp. 17–31, and *Lettre sur une inscription du cloître de Moissac,* ibid, IX, 1853, pp. 390–397. Francis Pottier, *L'abbaye de St.-Pierre à Moissac,* in *Album des Monuments et de l'Art Ancien du Midi de la France,* Toulouse, Privat, 1893–1897, I, pp. 49–63. Jules Momméja, *Mosaïques du Moyen-Age et Carrelages émaillés de l'abbaye de Moissac,* in *Bulletin Archéologique,* Paris, 1894, pp. 189–206. Viré, Chenet, and Lemozi, *Fouilles exécutées dans le sous-sol de Moissac en 1914 et 1915,* in *Bull. de la Soc. Archéol. de Tarn-et-Garonne,* XLV, 1915, pp. 137–153. *Addendum et rectification,* ibid, pp. 154–158. For the excavations of 1930, conducted by M. Viré, see the report in the *Comptes Rendus de l'Académie des Inscriptions et Belles-Lettres,* 1930, pp. 360, 361.

40. *L'abbaye et les cloîtres de Moissac,* Paris, Picard, 1897. Mention is made of an illustrated work by J. M. Bouchard, *Monographie*

de l'église et du cloître de Saint-Pierre de Moissac, Moissac, 1875, but it has been inaccessible to me.

41. *Congrès Archéologique de France*, Paris, Picard, 1902, pp. 303–310 (by Brutails). The congress of 1865 also visited Moissac and reported the discovery of fragments of another cloister. See Rupin, *op. cit.*, p. 200, and Legrèze-Fossat, *op. cit.*, III, pp. 107, 108.

42. There is a brief report in the *Bulletin Archéologique*, Paris, 1903, p. li.

43. *L'art religieux de XIIe siècle en France*, Paris, Colin, 1922, and *Les influences arabes dans l'art roman*, in *Revue des Deux Mondes*, Nov. 15, 1923, pp. 311–343.

44. *Notes sur la sculpture romane en Languedoc et dans le nord de l'Espagne*, in *Bulletin Monumental*, 1923, pp. 305–351; *L'autel roman de Saint-Sernin de Toulouse et les sculpteurs de cloître de Moissac*, in *Bulletin Archéol.*, Paris, 1923, pp. 239–250, pls. XIX-XXVII; *Les débuts de la sculpture romane en Languedoc et en Bourgogne*, in *Revue Archéologique*, Paris 5e série, XIX, 1924, pp. 163–173; *Notes sur la sculpture romane en Bourgogne*, in *Gazette des Beaux-Arts*, 5e période, VI, 1922, pp. 61–80.

45. *Romanesque Sculpture of the Pilgrimage Roads*, Boston, Marshall Jones, 1923, 10 volumes; *Spain or Toulouse? and other Questions*, in *Art Bulletin*, VII, 1924, pp. 1–25; *Leonesque Romanesque and Southern France*, ibid, VIII, 1926, pp. 235–250.

46. The sculptures of Moissac have been discussed also by Wilhelm Vöge, *Die Anfänge des monumentalen Stiles im Mittelalter*, Strassburg, Heitz, 1894; Albert Marignan, *Histoire de la sculpture en Languedoc du XIIe-XIIIe siècle*, Paris, Bouillon, 1902; Gabriel Fleury, *Études sur les portails imagés du XIIe siècle*, Mamers, 1904; André Michel, in his *Histoire de l'Art*, I, 2e partie, Paris, Colin, 1905, pp. 589–629 (*La sculpture romane*); Jean Laran, *Recherches sur les proportions dans la statuaire française du XIIe siècle*, in *Revue Archéologique*, 1907, pp. 436–450; 1908, pp. 331–358; 1909, pp. 75–93, 216–249; Auguste Anglès, *L'abbaye de Moissac*, Paris, Laurens, 1910; Robert de Lasteyrie, *L'architecture religieuse en France à l'époque romane*, Paris, Picard, 1912, pp. 640 ff.; Ernst Buschbeck, *Der Portico de la Gloria von Santiago de Compostella*, Wien, 1919, pp. 24 ff.; J. Jahn, *Kompositionsgesetze französicher Reliefplastik im 12. und 13. Jahrhundert*, 1922, pp. 11–16; Alfred Salmony, *Europa-Ostasien, religiöse Skulpturen*, Potsdam, Kiepenheuer,

1922; Raymond Rey, *La cathédrale de Cahors et les origines de l'architecture à coupoles d'Aquitaine*, Paris, Laurens, 1925, *Les vieilles églises fortifiées du Midi de la France*, Paris, Laurens, 1925, and *Quelques survivances antiques dans la sculpture romane méridionale*, in *Gazette des Beaux-Arts*, 5e période, XVIII, 1928, pp. 173–191.

47. Charles Rufus Morey, *The Sources of Romanesque Sculpture*, in *Art Bulletin*, II, 1919, pp. 10–16; *Romanesque Sculpture*, Princeton, 1920; *The Sources of Mediaeval Style*, in *Art Bulletin*, VII, 1924, pp. 35–50.

[47a. On Mâle's ideas concerning Moissac see my article: "Two Romanesque Drawings in Auxerre and some iconographic problems," *Studies in Art and Literature for Belle da Costa Greene*, Princeton, 1954, pp. 331–349, reprinted in my *Selected Papers*, vol. I, *Romanesque Art*, 1977, pp. 306–327.]

48. For the appearance of the buildings prior to the restorations, see the lithographs and engravings in Nodier, Taylor, and de Cailleux, *op. cit.*, I, partie 2, 1834, pl. 65, and Rupin, *op. cit.*, pp. 199, 200, figs. 34, 35. In the early nineteenth century the galleries were covered by wooden barrel vaults, and several capitals and columns in the west and north galleries were then replaced or enclosed by piers of rectangular section. These must have been later substitutions which were removed in the 1840s by the French restorers of the cloister. The present columns and capitals are contemporary with the others. In only one of them (number 61) is there an exceptional form—a greater breadth of the astragal and thicker columns—which may be explained by the fact that the arch of the lavatorium sprang from this very capital. See below, n. 68.

49. Except the central pier of the south gallery which is a monolith of reddish marble. Lagrèze-Fossat, *op. cit.*, III, p. 259, has mistakenly described all the piers as monoliths. The revetment is a thin hollowed marble case with two or three unjointed sides. The fourth side is stuccoed or faced with a thin slab of marble (central western pier, Fig. 27).

50. The height of the piers, without their imposts and podia, ranges from 1.57 m. to 1.60. The angle piers are not quite square in section, and vary in breadth from .49 m. (St. John, Fig. 16) to .53 (St. Paul, Fig. 12). The central pier of the east gallery (abbot Durand, Fig. 13) is .72 m. wide on its east and west faces, and .52 m. deep. The central north pier (unsculptured) is .66 m. by .51 m., the central west, with the inscription (Fig. 24) and St. Simon

(Fig. 27), is .69 m. by .52; but the relief of Simon, set in the broader side, is only .51 m. wide. The thickness of the slabs is no more than .04 to .05 m. (in those piers of which the narrow edge of a slab is exposed). On the southwest and northwest piers the slabs were too narrow to cover the sides on which are sculptured Philip and Matthew (Fig. 22); extremely slender pieces were added to complete the revetment. In the relief of Philip (Fig. 23) a vertical joint runs along the right column and cuts the arch. His mantle has been designed parallel to this line, and never crosses it; and a wide interval has been left between the O and L of APOSTOLUS in the inscription to avoid crossing this same joint.

51. The figure of Simon (Fig. 27) was for many years enwalled in the exterior of the south porch of the church, where it was seen by Dumège (before 1823) and the authors of the *Voyages pittoresques et romantiques* (before 1834). It was restored to its present position by Viollet-le-Duc or his assistant, Olivier, during the restorations of the 1840s. It is not certain that it is now in its original place, but it undoubtedly belonged to the cloister. That all the apostles were once represented cannot be inferred from the structure of the piers. The central southern pier is intact. Of the two remaining piers with blank faces, the central northern has, on its south side, a brick filling up to the very edge of the impost. Unless this is a more recent change it would exclude the application of a slab to its one bare surface. The same holds true of the central eastern pier (Durand), for the marble encloses the two narrow sides completely, and there is no place on the broader (west) side with exposed brick surface for a marble slab. Hence it must be concluded that only nine apostles (including Paul) were originally represented on the piers. Others were perhaps carved on the corner pier of the destroyed lavatorium or fountain enclosure (see below, n. 68), and on the supports of some adjacent monastic structure. It is possible, however, that narrower slabs (c. 51 m.), of the same dimensions as those of the corner piers, were once inserted on these broader faces (.66 m., .72 m.) of the central piers. The relief of Simon (.51 m) is narrower than that of Durand (.72 m.).

52. For similar treatment of hair in archaic Greek sculpture, see Lechat, *Au musée de l'acropole d'Athènes*, Paris, 1903, fig. 5 (p. 99), fig. 7 (p. 125), fig. 33 (p. 343).

53. After his death he appeared in a dream to a monk of Cluny, with his mouth swollen with saliva and unable to speak. Six monks had to maintain a vigil of absolute silence in order to redeem him. See Migne, Patr. lat. CLIX, col. 873, 901, 913.

54. There is a similar distortion in drawings in the Gospels of Matilda of Tuscany, an Italian manuscript contemporary with the cloister. It is now in the Pierpont Morgan Library. See *Gospels of Matilda Countess of Tuscany, 1055–1115*, with an Introduction by Sir George Warner. Privately printed, Roxburghe Club, 1917, pl. XXIV.

55. The costume of Bartholomew (Fig. 21) is also misunderstood. Note the misplaced buckle and the false mantle on the right shoulder. With his left hand he holds up the bottom of his tunic—a common gesture in the capitals—which covers still another tunic. The diagonal of the outer tunic is obviously classical, and the gesture of the saint appears to be a rationalization of that diagonal. The lower edges of the costume of Philip (Fig. 23) are also arbitrary and unclear.

56. Cf. the Amazon Hippolyta in the relief from Martes-Tolosanes, near Toulouse—Esperandieu, *Recueil général des bas-reliefs de la Gaule romaine*, II, fig. 5, p. 37.

57. As on the capitals of the south transept portal of Saint-Sernin in Toulouse, dated before 1093.

58. The tympanum of the aisle portal of Saint-Sernin. The smooth unincised eye occurs also at Chartres—Houvet, *Cathédrale de Chartres, Portail Royal*, pl. 28.

59. Cf. W. Deonna, Les "Apollons Archaiques," Geneva, 1909, p. 24, n. 2. The oblique axis of the eyes of Paul, Simon, Andrew, and John is also a feature of archaic Greek art.

60. Note especially the forms of B, R T, h, and O, as well as the sign of contraction, with its central handle; and the use of superposed circular dots instead of triangular notches.

61. See below, p. 68.

62. I have considered above the linear design. But these sculptures were originally painted, and their effect depended also on the color which distinguished areas, accented parts, and possibly determined patterns not suggested by the carving we see today. Traces of color—pinkish and greenish tints—are still visible on the apostles. But they are so faint and fragmentary that little can be inferred from them as to the original scheme of painting. They seem to have been clearer seventy years ago when the figures were described by Viollet-le-Duc (*Dictionnaire*, VIII, p. 111).

63. If we follow the courses of the concentric folds incised in clear sets on the mantle of Peter, on his arms, and on the torso between the arms, we shall observe that they form three distinct sets of intercepted lines, detached from each other.

64. The lozenge ornament of the enriched portions of the costume is also significant in its zigzag and unstable units. A sculptor of more classic style would have used beads or another circular motif.

65. The frequency of angular letters is also characteristic.

66. Cf. also with the inscription recording the completion of the cloister in 1100 (Fig. 24). It begins with several lines of small letters, close-packed, linked, crossed, and nested in unpredictable groupings, and ends with a series of large, regularly spaced letters in four uniform rows of repeated initials in sets of three: V.V.V./ M.D.M./R.R.R./F.F.F.—a remarkable contrast of script styles.

[These enigmatic letters, which have engaged the curiosity of local antiquarians who mistakenly read them in vertical sequence (see Rupin, *op. cit.*, p. 315), are a variant of an inscription of mysterious alliterative initials often found in manuscripts since the ninth century and interpreted there as a prophecy of the fall of Rome. In some instances the decipherment is attributed to Bede. V.V.V. is read as Venit Victor Validus or Victor Vitalis Veniet, M.M.M. as Monitus Monumentum Mortuus (sic), R.R.R. as Rex Romanorum Ruit, F.F.F. as Ferro Frigore Fame. On this mediaeval puzzle, which seems to have arisen from the effort to decipher an inscription on a Roman monument, see the instructive article by Karl-August Wirth "Überlieferung und Illustration eines mittelalterlichen Anekdotenstoffes," *Münchner Jahrbuch der bi'denden Kunst*, XII, 1961, pp. 46–64, including on pp. 54–55 and in notes 75, 76 interesting observations by Professor Bernhard Bischoff. The inscription in Moissac has been overlooked in the writings on this subject.]

67. The variation in the size of the capitals—some single capitals having a greater vertical dimension—indicated by Taylor and Rupin (Rupin, *op. cit.*, fig. 38) is sporadic rather than systematic. It appears in only a few capitals. But the single columns, with a few exceptions, have a greater diameter than the twin (.165 m., 13 m.).

68. The existence of the lavatorium is inferred from the traces of arches above the central pier of the north gallery and the fifth capital from the northwest pier in the west gallery—both arches springing toward the garden of the cloister. Since a fountain once stood in this northwest corner of the cloister the inference seems even better founded. Lenoir, in his *Architecture Monastique*, Paris, 1856, p. 312, fig. 469, reproduced an engraving of the marble basin of the fountain, after an "old drawing" of which he unfortunately did not state the provenance. That this fountain was an elaborate, perhaps richly sculptured construction, is implied in the description by the abbot Aymeric de Peyrac (c. 1400), "*quidem lapis fontis marmoreus et lapis medius portalis* [the trumeau], *inter ceteros lapides harum precium, reputantur pulcherrima magnitudine et subtilli artificio fuisse constructi, et cum magnis sumptibus asportati et labore*" (Chronicle, f. 160 vo., col. I, Rupin, p. 66, n. 2). He attributed both works to the abbot Anquêtil (1085–1115), who built the cloister. The fountain was observed in the seventeenth century by a traveler, Leon Godefroy (see note 29 above). A fountain with an arcaded enclosure of the late Romanesque period exists in the cloister of San Zeno in Verona (A. Kingsley Porter, *Lombard Architecture*, IV, pl. 234, 4).

Lagrèze-Fossat, *op. cit.*, III, p. 265, has denied the existence of such an enclosure in Moissac, especially since the traces of the arches are in the same brick as the arches of the cloister and belong to the later thirteenth century. He states that excavation has revealed no trace of the foundations and suggests that a lavatorium enclosure was undertaken in the thirteenth century but never completed. He overlooked the exceptional breadth of the lower part of the capital of the west gallery (Annunciation to the Shepherds and Daniel between the lions, Figs. 32, 86), which received the springs of this lavatorium arch, and also the existence in Moissac of a series of capitals and colonnettes of the same material and dimensions as those of the cloister. They are now in the Belbèze estate, which is on the grounds of the monastery. The Belbèze family occupies the old palace of the abbots of Moissac. The slight foundation required for such an arcade might have been removed with the arcades themselves, especially since the garden of the cloister was cultivated, and in the nineteenth century served as the dumping ground of a saltpeter establishment.

69. Rupin, *op. cit.*, fig. 37, reproduce after Nodier and Taylor, a view of what has been called both the *petit* and *grand cloître*—a galleried enclosure that occupied the site of the Petit Seminaire of Moissac. Its pointed arches of simple rectangular section were carried by twin tangent colonnettes. It is difficult to judge from the old lithograph the date of this building; it is presumably a Gothic

construction. Fragments of this cloister were observed by the archaeological congress which visited Moissac in 1865 (Rupin, *op. cit.*, p. 200, Lagrèze-Fossat, *op. cit.*, III, p. 107). They consisted of the remains of a single bay with unsculptured capitals and two marble columns engaged to a pier.

70. The combined diameters of the astragals are a little more than .41 m., whereas on most of the twin capitals their breadth ranges from .32 to .36. A similar proportion appears in the Adoration of the Magi (Fig. 58) and an ornamented capital in the west gallery—the fourth from the south pier—of which the breadth of the astragal on the longer sides is .40 m.

71. The same figure rarely appears twice on a single side of a capital. An exception is the Virgin in the Annunciation and Visitation (Figs. 31, 66).

72. This variant of the continuous method in mediaeval art was overlooked by Dagobert Frey in his excellent *Gotik und Renaissance*, 1930, in which he distinguishes early mediaeval space and representation as successive and those of the Renaissance as simultaneous. He has identified the order of the represented objects (content) with the order of the design, although these may be distinct.

73. Interesting for the freely composed rather than strictly narrative successive character of Romanesque illustration is the grouping of incidents on the tympanum of Bourg-Argental (Porter, *Romanesque Sculpture of the Pilgrimage Roads*, 1923, ill. 1150), where the scenes are ordered from right to left, but the figures within these scenes move from left to right.

74. Cf. also the diagonal sides of the building in Cana (Fig. 30). In Lazarus and Dives (Fig. 68) the corner tower cuts the adjacent building diagonally.

75. In the Washing of Feet (Fig. 75) the name of Peter is incised in his nimbus from right to left. It is the symmetrical counterpart of the name of Christ who kneels before him at the left. The reversal of direction produces a pairing of names analogous to the grouping of the two figures. I mention here, as of possible significance to those who might seek an iconographic interpretation of this reversal, the existence of a retrograde inscription to St. Peter in the lapidary museum of Béziers in Languedoc (J. D., *L'Histoire de Béziers racontée par ses pierres—Catalogue du Musée Lapidaire*, Béziers, Barthe, 1912, pl. XXIV, fig. 1). See also note 82 below. The inscription of Nero in the martyrdom of Paul (Fig. 87) is also reversed; it corresponds to the scepter on the left side.

76. The decomposition of words in the most archaic capitals of the cloister corresponds to the decorative distortion or realignment of the separate abstracted elements of an object. The word as an incised composite whole, of which the elements could be freely rearranged to make new words, had, perhaps, no rigid axis to an archaic artist; its elements, the letters, stood in no fixed relation to the whole, and could be arranged freely, except where a specific combination (the monogram of Christ) had a symbolic value. Another archaism in the inscriptions of the cloister is the reversal of N and S even in normal inscriptions—a practice common in the writing of children and the newly literate. It is also characteristic of the archaic indeterminacy of the form of S and N, which have two diagonal axes—one explicit, the other implied—that in the reversed inscription, mentioned above, the final S has been detached from the word and written in its normal direction between the two goats, and that in the reversed inscription of Nero (Fig. 87) only the N remains normal.

77. Note the lotuslike plant on which the saints and angels repose—a remarkable parallel to Chinese Buddhist sculptures which also present such groupings of figures on a mandorla-shaped surface.

78. A head inserted between the two apostles at the left balances the accent on the figures of Christ and the Virgin at the right.

79. The ornament of the impost also participates in this conception, through so remote from it in content. Despite its involve-

ment and interlaced birds, the ornament of the lower band is divided symmetrically. The birds diverge from a central mascaron of which they grasp the divergent horns as the angel grasps the hands of John.

80. There is an especially subtle example in the Martyrdom of Saturninus (Figs. 43, 53). Here the design of adjacent faces is related by common diagonal directions.

81. Note, however, the contrast of gesture and head in the figures before the king in the capital of the Martyrdom of St. Saturninus (Fig. 43) in the east gallery.

82. When this master of the south gallery reversed an inscription in the capital of David and the Musicians, it was not designed to produce the simple decorative symmetry of the archaic capitals of the cloister, but a more intricate opposition. For words in the normal direction are placed directly underneath the reversed names. Thus in the inscription ASAPH CVm LIRA, the first two words are incised from right to left, the third from left to right immediately below. In the inscription EMAN CVM ROTA, EMan is reversed and the following words are written below in the normal order. Is the reversal in this instance possibly influenced by the wish to imitate the direction of Hebrew letters? It is unlikely, even though the conception of this subject is based on the preface to the psalter. In a Latin manuscript of the same period, a miniaturist of Moissac reproduced a Hebrew inscription on the scroll of Jeremiah (Bibl. Nat. lat. 1822).

83. In the density of the whole, in the multiplying of small contrasting elements and the movement of diagonal lines and surfaces, the foliate capitals share the Romanesque character analyzed in the pier reliefs.

84. *Bulletin Archéologique*, Paris, 1923, p. 247.

85. A more complex banding occurs in the south gallery in the Vision of John (Fig. 56).

86. There are exceptions, even in the very archaic capitals, like the Adoration of the Magi (Fig. 36). It is characteristic of such figures that their stance is very light, and that their feet are parallel, not normal to the background (Figs. 43, 112).

In the capital of Adam and Eve (Fig. 40) Adam and the Lord stand on little sloping pedestals, remnants of a separate private ground or hillock from late classical and early mediaeval art. They are the clearest sign of the absence of a general concept or abstraction of a common ground plane in these sculptures.

87. In the Washing of Feet no seats at all are represented behind the figures. The application of the vertical projection described above to human figures may be seen in the capitals of Lazarus and Dives (Fig. 67), St. Laurence (Fig. 80), and Benedict (Fig. 41) in representations of recumbent bodies.

88. In the capitals of the three Marys at the Tomb in Issoire, the three soldiers are similarly superposed, but in alternating directions.

89. This is especially clear in the representation of the innkeeper in the doorway on the capital of the Good Samaritan (Fig. 59).

90. A related succession of surfaces, with a similar archaic parallelism, appears in the Chaining of the Dragon (Fig. 58).

91. Several figures in the east gallery hold up the edges of their tunics or mantles like Bartholomew (Fig. 21). In the Washing of Feet James has the melon cap of the apostle John on the northeast pier (Fig. 16).

92. But in some capitals, portions of the head invisible to the spectator are carved in detail (Nero, Fig. 87).

93. The angel who takes the soul of Paul at his martyrdom (not reproduced) is also represented in profile. Cf. also the seated Christ washing the feet of Peter (Fig. 75).

94. On the same capital an apostle is placed between Christ and the Canaanite woman; the conversation thereby becomes indirect and more complicated. For the use of a more developed type of gesturing figure in the east gallery, cf. Fig. 43, of the Martyrdom of Saturninus. This is one of the most refined capitals in the east gallery.

95. The inscription of the impost of Nebuchadnezzar (Fig. 47) includes the crossed and enclosed letters of the inscription of 1100 (Fig. 24).

96. Raymond Rey, *La cathédrale de Cahors*, Paris, Laurens, 1925, pp. 120 ff.

97. Wilhelm Vöge, *Die Anfänge des monumentalen Stiles im Mittelalter*, Strassburg, 1894, pp. 267 ff. (270, n. 5, on Moissac).

98. A. Venturi, *Storia dell' arte italiana*, I, fig. 79.

99. A similar analysis could be made of the two adjoining elders at the ends of the upper row.

100. The text describes the elders as seated in a circle about Christ—*in circuitu sedis*. This spatial conception, which was observed by mediaeval commentators and interpreted mystically, has been projected vertically on the wall of the tympanum.

101. There is a slight bending of the legs of the seraphim.

102. For an analogous turn of the head in a figure looking directly upwards, see Lauer, *Les enluminures romanes de la Bibliothèque Nationale*, Paris, 1926, pl. XXXII—a miniature of the mid-eleventh century from St.-Germain-des-Prés (Bibl. Nat. lat. 11550).

103. Barrière-Flavy, *Les arts industriels des peuples barbares de la Gaule*, Toulouse, Privat, 1901, I, pp. 75–80. The native Celt-Iberic population are often beardless in the Roman reliefs—cf. Déchelette, *Manuel d'archéologie préhistorique*, II, *Archéologie celtique ou protohistorique*, pt. 3, Paris, 1914, p. 1582; and Ésperandieu, *Recueil des bas-reliefs de la Gaule romaine*, 9 vols., 1907–1928, *passim*.

104. Cf. Saint-Gall ms. 51—Beissel, *Geschichte der Evangelienbücher*, Freiburg i. Br., 1906, fig. 33. For examples in Irish sculpture, see H. S. Crawford, *Handbook of Carved Ornament from Irish Monuments of the Christian Period*, Dublin, 1926, pl. L.

105. Porter, *Romanesque Sculpture of the Pilgrimage Roads*, Boston, 1923, ills. 434, 435.

106. *Ibid*, fig. 359.

107. R. Hamann, *Deutsche und französische Kunst im Mittelalter*, I, 1923, fig. 107. A similar treatment of the hair in a figure in the Duomo of Ferrara—*ibid*, fig. 104.

108. Porter, *Spanish Romanesque Sculpture*, New York, 1928, I, pl. 35.

109. E. Houvet, *La cathédrale de Chartres, Portail Royal*, pls. 18, 26.

110. Porter, *Romanesque Sculpture of the Pilgrimage Roads*, ill. 697. There is an example in S. Clements, Santiago—a figure of a prophet in the style of Master Mateo.

111. As in the Last Judgment of the portal of Bourges cathedral. In the legend of Turkill, the hero, passing through Paradise, observed that "Adam was smiling with one eye and weeping with the other; smiling at the thought of those of his descendants who would find eternal life, and weeping at the thought of those destined to damnation." (From M. P. Asin, *Islam and the Divine Comedy*, London, 1926, p. 200.)

112. In the early Romanesque sculptures of Moissac the folds are primarily pleats, in later art, creases.

113. Ésperandieu, *Recueil*, II, p. 309, no. 411.

114. Lechat, *Au musée de l'acropole d'Athènes*, Paris, 1903, fig. 29; K. With, *Die asiatische Plastik*, pl. 27.

115. Reinach, *Repertoire de reliefs Grecs et Romains*, Paris, 1909, I, pp. 223, 224 (Phigaleia); Ésperandieu, *Recueil*, IV, p. 201.

116. A. Boinet, *La miniature carolingienne*, Paris, 1913, pl. 20.

117. Van Berchem and Clouzot, *Mosaïques chrétiennes*, Geneva, 1924, fig. 66.

118. O. Siren, *La sculpture chinoise de V^e au XIVe siècle*, Van Oest, Paris and Brussels, 1925, pls. 3–11.

119. The two outer rosettes are cut unequally by the edges of the lintel.

120. This stepping is perhaps also a stylistic bias in the technique. Its practice in Islamic art (joggled lintels) may throw light on the practice in France.

121. In Beaulieu, Martel, Souillac, Cahors and the manuscripts of Limoges.

122. The fourth and seventh from the left.

123. *L'abbaye de Moissac*, Paris, Laurens, 1910, pp. 28, 29.

124. I have discussed the history of the lintel and the relation of its ornament to earlier arts in a paper read at the meeting of the College Art Association in December, 1928, and summarized in *Parnassus* I, 3, March, 1929, pp. 22, 23.

125. Cf. Rupin, *op. cit.*, p. 331.

126. The second Magus is cut vertically by the joint of two vertical slabs (Fig. 126). The reliefs were carved and set in place before the enclosing architecture was erected. This is a variation of the usual method, which has been little noticed in discussions of the techniques of sculpture *avant* and *après la pose*. The hand of the first Magus is obscured by the central capital, and on the adjoining relief (Fig. 127) the head of the ass projects into the haunch of the arch, which has been specially cut to admit this head.

In the capitals of the porch, unlike those of the cloister, there is no longer a limiting structure of volutes, consoles, and central triangular frame. Their carving shapes an irregular, broadly conical surface without division into four distinct fields, and is so deeply cut that the background is hardly apparent and the figures cannot be regarded as a *decoration* of the capital.

127. Even the arcaded bays of the side walls are not strictly symmetrical or regular, but are deliberately designed to produce an alternation of unequal parts (Figs. 120, 121). On the east wall, the south bay is the broader, on the west wall, the north. Each bay is divided into four slabs, two above and two below—but slabs of unequal breadth, arranged in symmetrical alternation.

128. These scales led de Lasteyrie to suppose that the slabs were reemployed lids of Early Christian sarcophagi. But in this he was mistaken, for not only do their dimensions disagree with those of the early sarcophagi of the region, but the units are also considerably smaller than in the latter. In their tonguelike rather than semicircular form they resemble the scaly slabs on the gables of Aquitaine churches. The imbrications are carved on only four of the twelve slanting surfaces above the trefoils, and in one case (the Visitation) they adjoin the representation of arched windows and oculi. These show clearly enough that the imbricated ornament is designed to represent a rooftop and is not a remnant of the original decoration of a reemployed slab.

129. The great contrast in the sizes of the different figures of the same relief in Romanesque sculpture (Moissac, Vézelay, Autun) is an analogy in surface composition to the Baroque exaggeration of perspective diminutions and the frequent placing of a large figure in the immediate foreground and a very small one behind him. Such Baroque contrasts are not merely the result of a scientific perspective, but are designed to produce a strong and immediate opposition of adjacent objects and a precipitate movement in space. [I was not aware, when I wrote this, of the already current characterization of sixteenth-century works with these features as "Mannerist."]

130. In the sculptures of the facade of Ripoll, in Catalonia, the scenes move from left to right in superposed rows until the uppermost, where the direction is reversed.

131. Each of the four slabs of the frieze is designed as a balanced relief. The joint which divides the angel's body falls along the ass's tail, but although this is the central jointing of the frieze, the true vertical mid-line corresponds to the back of the mounted Virgin.

132. See note 126 above. The head is carved *in the slab*, which projects into the space enclosed by the arch, and also into the arch.

133. More than fifteen centimeters. Cf. the four or five centimeters of the reliefs of the cloister.

134. Laran (*Revue Archéologique*, 1907, pp. 436–450; 1908, pp. 331–358; 1909, pp. 75–93, 216–249) showed by the application of statistical anthropometric method to the study of the proportions of a large number of Romanesque figures that within any school of French Romanesque sculpture there exist two sets of proportions, one for large figures and another for small. He verified the apparent stylistic homogeneity of certain distinct groups (Languedoc, Bur-

gundy, Auvergne) in showing that this homogeneity varied with the mean deviation of the proportions of the figures included in the group. His measurements of Moissac are not reliable for statistical treatment however, since of the more than two hundred figures of the cloister and the fifty or more of the portal we are not told which were selected for comparison. The elders of the tympanum and the figures of the cloister capitals are included as small figures and their proportions averaged, although this smallness is relative and the elders are three to four times as large as those of the capitals. Factors of time and individual style were also neglected by Laran who averaged, as of one school, the regional works of different style and period. But these errors of method, while they may discredit the tabulation for Languedoc, are less apparent in the treatment of other regions. Measurement of all the capitals in Moissac would probably confirm Laran's general conclusions, although it might alter his specific figures.

135. Cf. the figures of the apostles in the sculpture of the Last Supper in the cathedral of Naumburg (c. 1245?), reproduced by Panofsky, *Deutsche Plastik des XI. bis dem XIII. Jahrhundert*, pl. 93.

136. Note especially his leper's bell on the porch.

136a. The measurements above the base moldings are: left jamb, .87 m.; left doorway, 1.61 m.; trumeau, .72 m.; right doorway, 1.67 m.; right jamb, .81 m. The height of Peter is 1.54 m. (including the lion at his feet), of Isaiah, with his larger pedestal, 1.66 m., and the breadths of their slabs, respectively .46 m. and .43 m.

137. The scalloping of the jambs, which appears in other churches of southwestern France, should be distinguished from the polylobed arches of Romanesque and Islamic art. For while the individual scallops of the latter have a clear analogy to the arched form of the whole, the scalloping of the jambs produces a line in

active contrast to the rigid verticals of the jambs. It is a distinctly more restless, broken form, which classicist taste has found reprehensible in mediaeval art. By the application of such scalloping to a jamb beside a trumeau (less prominently scalloped in Moissac) the doorway becomes an asymmetrical architectural unit without the appearance of static support inherent in the common lintel-and-post construction. On the contrary, the doorposts in Moissac are animated members of which the movement is accented by the pleated ribbon meandering on the inner edges (Fig. 136)). The slender colonnettes engaged to these narrow sides of the jambs are also lobed and broken, in contradiction of the nature of the columnar member.

138. The strong, square cutting of the seraph's head reappears in Peter (Fig. 138), but in the latter the chief facial planes meet in a line parallel to the elongated axis of the head and not perpendicular to it, as on the tympanum. Peter's hair is wavy and restless and falls low upon the brow in the manner of the cloister and tympanum.

139. A French writer discovered in the succession of ascending animals on these jambs—fish, bird, quadruped, and St. Peter—a Romanesque anticipation of the theory of evolution. See the *Bulletin de l'Association Française pour l'Avancement des Sciences et Arts de Montauban*, 1902.

140. The scallops increase in span as they ascend. This produces a more dynamic succession and at the same time a more harmonious transition to the lintel. Note also that the scalloping is in contrast to the circular rosettes of the trumeau rather than concentric with them.

141. The colonnettes of the doorposts have a flatter, deeper scotia than those of the trumeau.

142. ". . . *quidem lapis fontis marmoreus et lapis medius portalis, inter ceteros lapides harum precium, reputantur pulcherrima magnitudine et subtilli artifficio fuisse constructi, et cum magnis sumptibus asportati et labore; ymo pocius extimantur miraculose ibidem fuisse* [*constructi*], *quod opere hominis, maxime unius simplicis abbatis.*" Chronicle, f. 160 vo., col. 1, Rupin, *op. cit.*, p. 66, n. 2. On the marble font, see above, note 68.

143. Aymeric called them leopards, and observed the existence of a similar sculptured beast on the portal of a priory of Moissac in Cénac (near Périgueux), built by the abbot Anquêtil (1085–1115). The church survives, but without trace of such a sculpture. That it was a lion to the sculptor and not a leopard appears from a close resemblance to the lion of Mark in the tympanum. The identification of these two species in the Middle Ages is well illustrated in a manuscript of the twelfth century from La Charité (diocese of Besançon) now in the British Museum (Add. Ms. 15603); on f. 113 vo. marginal drawings of two very similar beasts are labeled *leo* and *lipar*. The text of Aymeric reads ". . . *perlegi fundacionem dicti prioratus* [Cénac] *per scripturas antiquas, et reperi quod ipse Asquilinus, seu ejus contemplacione et procuracione et secundum formam operis ecclesie patet, quod ipse fecerit quia de similibus operis et sculturis videtur esse artifficiatum, et in portali dicte ecclesie de Senaco est quidem leopardus, sicut in portali ecclesie Moyssiacy sculpatus.*" Chronicle, f. 159, vo., col. 2, f. 160 ro, col. 1, (cited by Rupin, *op. cit.*, p. 69, n. 9). [The nave and the portal of the church at Cénac have been rebuilt in the nineteenth century. The historiated capitals of the old choir show the same structure of volutes, console, and impost as those of the Moissac cloister.]

144. Paul has the posture of the seraphim of the tympanum; the prophet is similar to the Isaiah in Souillac, and more remotely to the angel of Matthew in the tympanum.

[145. These figures perhaps owe much of their dryness to a recutting in the nineteenth century.]

LIST OF ILLUSTRATIONS

Page references follow description.